T0209446

For Such a Time as This

Kampouris and Kairos

Mark Coppenger

WESTBOW
PRESS®
A DIVISION OF THOMAS NELSON
& ZONDERVAN

WestBow Press books may be ordered through booksellers or by contacting:

WestBow Press
A Division of Thomas Nelson & Zondervan
1663 Liberty Drive
Bloomington, IN 47403
www.westbowpress.com
1 (866) 928-1240

ISBN: 978-1-9736-3647-2 (sc)
ISBN: 978-1-9736-3648-9 (hc)
ISBN: 978-1-9736-3646-5 (e)

Library of Congress Control Number: 2018909715

Print information available on the last page.

WestBow Press rev. date: 8/30/2018

Contents

Acknowledgements

This book is an acknowledgement of the great blessing Mano and Camille Kampouris have been to me, both as instruments of God's providence in my life and through the people they've assembled for the range of projects described herein. I've found encouragement and inspiration from their whole team, and had my iron sharpened right along.

First, I'd like to mention here those who've been particularly helpful in the writing of this book. Of course, I must again mention the Kampourises, who've hosted me several times at their New York apartment, filling my notebooks and folders with good material, providing a range of documents and photos for my use (including invaluable notes on Mano's early life by Laura Florio, from whose work I drew heavily in the first chapter). They've been kind to work back and forth with me on successive drafts, with email exchanges and hours on the phone. Once they heard the book was structured to give God the glory for his superintendence of their lives and ministries, they were on board.

I'm grateful for the face-to-face interviews others have granted me: Herb London and Greg Thornbury in New York City; Brian Pinney in Dayton, Ohio; Bob Phillips in Ankeny, Iowa; Ben Mitchell and Jacob Shatzer in Jackson, Tennessee; Doug Baker in Philadelphia; and Greg Gilbert in Louisville. I'm also thankful for the hospitality given me in these connections, including dinner at the Mitchells and overnight lodging and meals at the Pinneys.

Thanks, too, goes to those who pitched in by email—Glenn Nisbett in Johannesburg; Shane Walker in Linthicum, Maryland; David Roach in Nashville; Peter Riddell in Melbourne; Aaron Menikoff in Atlanta; Nick Tucker in Birmingham, England; and Michael McClennahan in Belfast—and by phone—Karl Tiedeman and Eric Metaxas from New York City and Charles and Tricia Marnham from London.

As always, I'm so grateful to Sharon, my wife, who not only encouraged me in the writing of this book (and helped with proofing), but also who lived much of it, with frequent occasions to meet with the crew in New York. Let me also mention my daughter, Chesed, who joined the Marnhams in giving the draft a careful onceover and offering good suggestions.

Preface

In the summer of 2002, I was driving south on the "Tri-State," I-294 west of Chicago. Just north of O'Hare Airport, my cell phone rang, and I heard an unfamiliar voice, that of Doug Baker, calling on behalf of someone named Emmanuel Kampouris. As Southern Baptists sympathetic to the "conservative resurgence" (meant to restore trust in biblical inerrancy to the denomination's seminary faculties and agency staffs), Doug and I had worked in similar circles. But this wasn't a call exclusively about the interests of the Southern Baptist Convention; it was something more broadly evangelical.

At that moment, I was two and a half years into a church planting effort in Evanston, Illinois, just up the lake shore from Chicago. We were meeting Sunday mornings in the YWCA, and our congregation was made up largely of students from Northwestern University, where I also served as director of Baptist Collegiate Ministry. We had some financial support from friends and churches, and the denomination was pitching in some funds as well—enough to rent the space, print some material, have a phone line, provide some lunch-time fellowship meals, etc. But things were quite lean. Students weren't able to give much. (I recall a day when we had around fifty in church, with an offering under $40.) So, in that high-cost area, our family was scarcely managing on the income we could gain from Sharon's service as a school superintendent's secretary, my adjunct teaching at Wheaton, Trinity, and Elmhurst (as well as substitute teaching at two nearby high schools—Evanston Township and New Trier, a few miles north in Winnetka), and daughter Chesed's work in a variety of establishments, including Walker Brothers Pancake House in Wilmette (mentioned in the movie *Mean Girls*) and coffee shops on Central and Chicago Avenues in Evanston.

Baker asked if I might be willing fly to Washington, DC, for a "writers camp," where I would join with others in composing a few trial articles for a prospective website designed to help pastors engage the culture prophetically. He said they'd cover expenses and pay me $1,500 for the week. I'd stay in a B&B across from Capitol Hill Baptist Church (where we'd meet) and have a Library of Congress card for research. I didn't quite know what to make of it, but I gave it a go, and it turned out to be one of the most wonderful things that ever happened to me.

I'd done a fair amount of writing and teaching for the church through the years, and some of that writing had gained me the invitation. The previous fall, Muslim terrorists had flown planes into the World Trade Center, and, even as the fallen towers were smoldering, Art Toalston from Baptist Press (BP) called to ask me to start writing on the matter, and I did so, submitting about twenty articles over the next month—a daily journal of reflection, if you will, from a variety of angles. Doug had passed one or more of these BP pieces along to Mr. Kampouris, and he thought I might be helpful to the team he was building.

As this book will tell, it's been quite a journey with the Kampourises, a journey that included a dinner-time conversation with Mrs. Kampouris (Camille) in January 2016. We were seated together at a square of tables arranged for our crew of fifteen or so at the Union Club on East 69th in New York. We'd all gotten to know each other pretty well over the years—fourteen years in my case—but that evening I heard something new—that she had dated Jerry Seinfeld for a bit. Already familiar with much of her life, as well as Mano's (Mr. Kampouris's nickname, which I ventured to use only after years of association), I pressed her, "Camille, you ought to write this stuff up." She responded, to my surprise, "Why don't you?"

To this off-handed remark, I smiled, shook my head, and let her know how far-fetched the idea was. So, we went on to talk about other things and to other people. However, over the next few days, an idea about how such a book could come to be began to arise in my mind, and I mentioned it to Mano and Camille in an email. I said I wasn't looking for work—particularly this sort—but I'd float an idea by them. They said "yes" to it.

My concept was to trace the work God had done to and through them thanks to some providential encounters—some "divine appointments"—that reset the course of their lives. The accomplishments noted would be substantial, but the glory would go to God for nudging (or jerking) them first one way and then another for his purposes. About a dozen of these forks in the road came to mind immediately. Since then, the list captured in the following chapters has grown to eighteen. Of course, I could have gone with fewer or more, for God's handiwork can be traced in many ways, but these have fallen out to me in my thinking and thanking.

One theme I chose to examine is the way in which the Kampourises have blessed so many people's lives and ministries through employment. My own story is a strong case in point. Though I'd played a number of visible and even celebrated roles in the preceding decades—as professor, pastor, and denominational leader—I was in an economically tough (albeit spiritually gratifying) spot when they called. We Coppengers weren't at all sure how we were going to hang in there financially and do right by our daughter who was heading off to college. But the Lord used them to put us on a firm financial footing and expand our reach beyond what we could have imagined.

So yes, enjoy this rehearsal of their accomplishments—through conferences, websites, films and such—but know that a great deal of the fruit can be seen in the lives and ministries of the dozens of "nobodies" they enlisted to work for and with them on astonishing projects. While they were investing in a wide range of ministries, they were also investing in a wide range of people enlisted to advance these causes.

The story begins in pre-World War II Egypt and England and takes us up to and through the present as we look at projects in the works. Along the way, we'll see the remarkable, separate journeys (both professional and spiritual) of Mano and Camille; their providential meeting after the tragic death of Myrto Kampouris, the wife of Mano's youth and the mother of his children; their energetic, imaginative, and steadfast collaboration and leadership on such projects as *Kairos Journal* (which I've served as managing editor) and *BibleMesh.*

There's much to tell, and sometimes I'll need to get ahead of myself, since I group particular events with their fruit, and the branches of nearby trees sometimes overlap. But I trust, in the end, it will all be sorted out. So, following the words of Esther 4:14 (the same words emblazoned on the *Kairos Journal* logo), we begin the story of a couple who has stepped forward under God in Christ "for such a time as this."

MANO

CHAPTER 1

"Welcome to the King's School!"
(From the Nile to Oxford and Back)

The bigger and older James Orr called the thirteen-year-old Emmanuel "Mano" Kampouris a *dago*, and in the ensuing scuffle, James punched Mano in the nose. Welcome to the King's School!

Kampouris's first days as a "foreigner" at this boarding school in Bruton, Somerset, England, were not particularly pleasant, for even though he spoke the King's English, he was counted something of a lesser being. Ironically, Kampouris was more cosmopolitan and urbane than Orr, his "superior," having grown up speaking five languages and assimilating elements of the cultures these tongues shaped and served. On that first day, those advantages didn't lessen the pain in his nose. However, in Kampouris's case, even this small, painful episode was beneficially formative, for it presented a *krisis*—a test that demonstrated and strengthened his steadfastness. It helped secure his resolve in what would prove to be a season of critical preparation for Christian impact, an eventuality he could not suspect at the time. Instead of calling home for relief, seeking escape, or withdrawing into a cocoon, he rose to meet the competition.

Kampouris would have to persist, and he did. He soon established himself as a leader in sports and earned cheers rather than taunts from his classmates. He passed the test of resiliency and proved his mettle, which was not an easy task for a teenager living as a stranger on a continent more than two thousand miles away from his family.

When we speak of "providential junctures" or "divine appointments," most people think of positive occurrences or happy occasions—an encouraging word or a personal introduction leading to fresh insight and accomplishment. But God uses all sorts of experiences, even seeming tragedies, to set us on our way toward blessing and fruitfulness. The Bible is full of examples: the crucifixion of Jesus gave us the Atonement; the stoning of Stephen launched the Christian diaspora; the doctrinal confusion of Peter and Barnabas prompted Paul's epistle to the Galatians; the frustration of his plans for Asia kept Paul available to answer his missionary call to Europe; and Paul's early, disappointing work with John Mark helped mold that young man into a future gospel writer. In other words, under God's sovereignty, it all works for good for his children.

The Nile Delta

Emmanuel was born on December 14, 1934, to Andrew Kampouris, a prosperous Greek cotton merchant in Egypt, and his wife, Eurydice (Caralli), who was a concert pianist. Early on, Mano was also exposed to Italian, French, and English, and he took to these languages as well as to the Arabic spoken around him. He began his formal schooling at the Mansourah Greek School (in this Nile Delta city around sixty miles west of Port Said), and then, at age nine, he transferred to Victoria College's day school in Alexandria—an esteemed, Anglo-centric institution modeled after the British public school system, whose students included Hussein, the future king of Jordan, and Ibrahim, the future prince of Madagascar. His courses were in English, and his garb was classically British, with flannel cap, gray shorts, striped school tie, and a blazer bearing the VC badge.

His father watched his grades carefully and stressed hard work and integrity in all Mano did, including sports. A polo player and race-horse owner, Andrew had Mano on horseback by age five, riding trails along the Nile. He taught him to shoot at seven, and the two of them went hunting on weekends. Then, when the boy was ten, Andrew arranged fencing lessons, a sport at which Mano excelled.

His mother, a graduate of the Conservatory of Lausanne, practiced four hours a day in their home and played in venues around Alexandria. Though she was a devoted parent, she employed nannies to make sure Mano got the consistent attention he needed as a child. He scarcely remembers the first nanny, Anna, but at age five, he came under the care of Stavroula Vizazopoulou, who helped raise him until he left for school in England at thirteen. Not surprisingly, he had trouble pronouncing her name, so he went with "Mademoiselle," which came out as "Enezel." The name stuck.

Well-versed in Greek Orthodox theology and etiquette for young children, Enezel had a strong, formative influence on the young Kampouris. He well remembers her favorite exhortation, "Be nice, be polite, be helpful," and he recalls an expression of grateful tenderness he showed toward her. On a visit with his parents to the great pyramids of Giza when he was twelve, he spied an intricate brooch of sapphires and pearls and persuaded his father to help him purchase it for Enezel. She cherished it all her life, and upon her death she bequeathed it to Mano, who has it in his possession today.

In those days, World War II loomed over Egypt, and Mano remembers the sound of German bombs in Alexandria. Because of the war, the original Victoria College building was pressed into duty as a British naval and military hospital, so many of their classes were moved to the San Stefano Hotel and Casino and, later, to a confiscated Italian school. His father kept an escape plan handy, by which Mano and his mother might meet an uncle's ship at Port Said for transport to South Africa via the Suez Canal. Thanks, however, to British troops under Field Marshall Bernard Law Montgomery at El Alamein, seventy miles to the west of Alexandria, the Germans were turned back, and a more-or-less normal life was secured for the Kampouris family.

Fortunately, normal school life for Mano was a rehearsal for study in England, since Victoria College was similarly structured around "houses," each with its own housemaster, captains, and prefects. Discipline was stringent, with one particular headmaster renowned for his collection of "therapeutic" canes, which he displayed proudly in an antique cabinet. Since Victoria prided itself on civilized students, Mano needed a certificate of good behavior to gain entry, and the school authorities were determined to finish whatever civilizing work needed to be done on its enrollees. Thus, by parents, nanny, and Victoria College, he was prepared for life at the King's School in England, where he matriculated from 1948 until 1954.

Up to this point, Mano's exposure to the Christian faith was essentially through the Orthodox Church, through the liturgy of services the family attended, and through the nurture of Enezel. Furthermore, as his Greek passport indicated, he'd been baptized as an infant into the Greek Orthodox Church. (Indeed, the Orthodox rite is the default entry for all native Greeks, such that any other religion listed on official documents requires special application to the government.) Regard for this heritage stuck with him through the years and proved helpful in times of crisis, as when, for instance, he found solace and direction in the monastery at Mount Athos, where he devoted days to prayer. Though "glorifying and enjoying" God was not yet the animating focus of his life, he was steeped in admiration for the church and its basic teachings.

King's School

For Andrew, it was a troubling matter to send his son so far away to school, but the political situation in Egypt was dicey, and he wanted his son to have a stable, properly British education. Though the cotton business kept Andrew from visiting Mano in England, he wrote him weekly, and their many exchanges kept them close (and Mano's Greek up to speed). Still, the separation was a challenge to the young Kampouris, especially when his classmates enjoyed frequent contact with their nearby families.

Founded in 1519 during the reign of Henry VIII and granted royal status under Henry's son Edward VI, the King's School trained Mano in Latin, rhetoric, and the theology of the Church of England. Though the setting was new—the rural, rolling hills of Southwest England instead of the urban bustle of Alexandria—his two schools shared a devotion to academics and sports, features Mano found congenial.

The school was also prestigious, and many of its students came from affluent families. Still, frugality was a watchword in England's postwar days. Students were limited to two shillings a week in their first two years, an allowance which topped out at five shillings a week in their senior year. With his allotment, Mano bought the coupons needed for his candy, but he also could be generous, as when he exhausted his funds to buy a visiting cousin's ticket for the Underground (the subway).

King's was organized around boarding houses, and Mano was fortunate to reside in the original one, the Old House, which was most convenient to the classrooms. He rose through the leadership ranks from prefect to head of house, a position which gave him freedom from curfews. As he earned the administration's respect, he also gained the friendship of classmates, some inviting him to visit their family homes during Leave Sundays.

The boys slept fourteen to a room, and those not engaged in sports bathed only twice a week, with five boys using the same water. The uniforms consisted of gray flannel shirts and pants and a navy tie with blazer. In the postwar economy, food was rationed and limited primarily to porridge and potatoes, with the infamous "steak and kidney pie" (a conglomeration of leftovers) coming at week's end. Sunday dining featured horse meat.

Though the facilities were drab and the food uninspiring, the education was gratifying. Mano especially remembers the math instruction of Mr. Elly, the French classes with Mr. Flintock, and Scripture with Reverend Ashcroft. However, athletics were Mano's passion, and there was plentiful opportunity for a range of competitions, including rugby, field hockey, cricket, shooting, swimming, and tennis. His father, Andrew, had trained him in many of these contests and raised him to believe he could do anything he set his mind to.

As school fencing champion, he was part of team victories over Eton, making quite a stir in the day. Of course, fencing had its risks. On one occasion, an opponent's épée pierced Mano's protective vest, leaving a wound requiring stitches; he bears the scar to this day. Rugby also took its toll. During a particularly ugly game, an opponent broke Mano's nose, and his coach sent him off by bike to a hospital in Wincanton, seventeen miles distant, where a Czech war veteran performed flawless reconstructive surgery. In less perilous competition, his skill in shooting took him to the Bisley Cup, with targets at two hundred and five hundred meters. He lost by a single point among the top marksmen in England.

Occasionally, his mother "Dicky" visited him at school, and others of his extended family made contact from time to time. He remembers a special occasion when his cousin Nana and her parents came to England. They invited him to stay with them at the luxurious Savoy Hotel in London, where, after a grand dinner, and when the elders retired, he and Nana went out to the famous Edmundo Ros's Latin-music club on Regent Street. It was a welcome respite from the austere and strenuous life of school.

Vacations were joy, a time for reunion with his parents in Alexandria; in the Cypriot mountain villages of Platres and Prodromos, where Mano played tennis and went hunting with some of his father's friends; and eventually at a villa his father purchased on the French Riviera at Cap d'Antibes.

In his early years at King's, Mano traveled to and from England by a flying boat operated by British Overseas Aircraft Corporation (BOAC). The plane took off from the Nile in Cairo and flew to the Sicilian harbor at Syracuse, where it stopped overnight and refueled before continuing to the port of Southampton, England. Later on, more conventional air service did the job, with fueling stops in Rome.

Throughout these school years, Mano matured right along, and he ended strong. Completing high school at King's, he passed his "A Levels" in French and history, and at the prompting of his headmaster, Geoffrey Sale (who was also his rugby coach), he applied to Oxford, which required an entrance exam and a lengthy interview before a panel of six or seven judges. He passed and made his way to Oxford in the fall of 1954.

As for his faith, he developed a fondness for Anglican worship and the faith's perspective, which permeated the school, even while he retained his Orthodox ties. Little did he suspect he would one day play a role in encouraging and strengthening Anglicans who fought, against the tide of heterodoxy, to keep their church within the Christian fold. But more on this later.

Oxford

Enrolling in Christ Church (the college named by Henry VIII; the home of the Cathedral Church of the Diocese of Oxford; and alma mater of John Wesley, John Locke, and William Penn), Mano chose to study law. He studied feverishly, devoting less time to sports.

He also found the setting at Oxford much more comfortable. Unlike the houses at King's, each student at the prestigious school had a spacious room with a study, plus a "scout" who performed valet service—making his bed, doing his laundry, and running errands. Mano and a dozen other students on his staircase enjoyed the ministrations of Bob Beasley, a balding, smallish, prim-and-proper older man who wore a bowler hat and blue suit. Furthermore, the money allowance was more liberal, and the students could use the house phone to make international calls, an option exercised by a range of foreign classmates, including Birabong Kasemsri (a Thai prince) and

Ravi Menon (the youngest brother of Krishna Menon, India's future prime minister).

Andrew had promised Mano that if he refrained from smoking until he was eighteen, he would buy him a car. True to his word, he supplied him, in his sophomore year, a check for five hundred pounds, which covered the cost of a green, two-seater Austin Healey. Mano used it to make frequent trips to London, particularly to concerts at the Royal Festival Hall. And ever the competitor, he entered a Royal Automobile Club 24-hour rally with history student David Hall serving as navigator. Things were going well until—with Mano in third or fourth place—the car skidded on some snow and left the road. Hall hit his head on the console and needed some stitches, but neither he nor the car suffered permanent damage.

Mano's course of study in law required his attendance at two lectures a week, connected with eleven courses spread over nine terms or three years. His curriculum included Roman, constitutional, land, contract, tort, criminal, and international law, as well as jurisprudence. Between lectures, he met with his tutor, E.H. ("Teddy") Burn, who assigned and discussed readings and essays. Burn, a lecturer and prolific author ten years his senior, was a great help advising him which lectures to attend and what information was necessary to pass the dreaded two exams, "Responsions" (now "Law Mods") and "Degree" (now "Schools" or "Finals"). The first came after two terms and decided whether the student could continue. The second followed the third year of study. Both exams were written, and the finals lasted three days. Emmanuel Kampouris successfully negotiated the challenging tests and graduated in 1957.

Myrto

Throughout his days in England, Mano's love grew for a childhood friend, Myrto Stellatos, whom he first saw at age four on the day of her baptism in a Greek Orthodox Church. The daughter of Gerassimos Stellatos, a mercurial and argumentative architectural engineer, and the former Elly Thomaides, a lovely woman from a talented and wealthy Greek-Albanian family, Myrto spoke Greek, grew up in the Greek Orthodox Church, lived within the Alexandrian Greek community, and attended the French Catholic School, *Dame de Sion*.

Since the Kampouris and Stellatos families were friends, Mano was able to see Myrto on his school vacations, sometimes at parties, or among friends who would go out dancing together. She was a vivacious, popular beauty, and by his last year at Bruton, Mano was completely taken with her. They began to exchange love letters, and when Mano moved into his later years at Oxford, Myrto persuaded her parents to enroll her at Eastbourne Ladies' College, a secretarial school in England, where they could see each other occasionally, all in strict decorum and within the guidelines of the visiting policies of Eastbourne and Oxford. In the latter case, she was the guest of a family friend, John Peristyanis, a history of anthropology professor at the university, who invited Mano to visit her at their home.

Once a graduate and back in Egypt, Mano proposed, and on July 4, 1959, the couple was married in the Orthodox cathedral of Alexandria. It was a grand affair with the reception at the elegant Stellatos villa. For their honeymoon, they took BOAC's first jet aircraft, the de Havilland Comet, to Vienna, from which they toured Austria, with visits to Innsbruck and Salzburg.

Back in Egypt, the couple set up house in Mansourah. Mano began work for his father, but before long, he moved into the employ of Andrew's partner in Alexandria, Anderson Clayton. He and Myrto took up lodging at the Stellatos villa, where they'd had their wedding reception. Myrto quit her job and became a full-time homemaker and companion in Mano's work, traveling with him on business trips, picking out his ties, and otherwise being his devoted teammate.

In all this, God was preparing Emmanuel Kampouris for extraordinary achievement on an international stage. He was, so to speak, born into comfortable privilege and enjoyed the sort of provision few receive. This can be perilous, for, as it says in 1 Corinthians 1:26, few born into the cultural elite are represented in the Kingdom of God. But, as Selina, Countess of Huntingdon, demonstrated, there's room for some of them (a story we recount in *Kairos Journal*). This wealthy patron of both John Wesley's and George Whitefield's eighteenth-century revivals said she gave thanks for the letter 'M' since, without it, the Scripture would read that not "any" privileged people would be called.

One way God uses such people is by equipping them with great gifts, opportunities, protection, and inspiration for accomplishment and status, and then claiming them later in life for his strategic, explicitly-Christian work in the world. C. S. Lewis is a case in point. As we learn in *Surprised by Joy*, he was a respected Oxford don before he became a Christian. However, once the transaction had occurred, he proved to be a daunting instrument in the Lord's hand.

Similarly, God facilitated the rise of Emmanuel Kampouris as a formidable and wealthy businessman, only to claim his know-how, drive, and substance for apostolic projects.

CHAPTER 2

An Invitation from Uncle Dennis (The Shift to Ceramics)

The Greeks have a long and distinguished history in Egypt. Indeed, Alexandria is named for Alexander the Great, who conquered the region and founded the city in the fourth century BC. When he fell ill and died in 323 in Babylon, his kingdom was divided among his generals, with Ptolemy taking charge of Egypt. Thus, the country was a fixture of the Hellenistic world, which encompassed today's Greece, Turkey, Israel, Iraq, Iran, and the Nile Valley. (It was in this milieu that the New Testament was written in Greek.)

In 1952, Gamal Abdel Nasser helped overthrow the Egyptian monarch, King Farouk, and, in 1956, he was elected Egypt's second president, an office he held (with an increasingly authoritarian hand) until his death in 1970. Nasser led the nation down a socialist path and flexed Egypt's muscles in a variety of ways, including the appropriation of the Suez Canal and the call for pan-Arab unity under his leadership. He found willing partners in the Soviet Union—partners pleased to provide him with jet fighters and surface-to-air missiles. He also nationalized foreign holdings, including the Kampouris family's cotton farms. Mano then found himself at a transition point. In the upheaval, Myrto's uncle, Dennis Kanellatos, offered him a position in his vitreous stoneware company in Alexandria. They made 36-inch sewer pipes, which were vitrified by throwing salt into the kiln, making them acid-resistant.

They also made refractory materials—bricks resistant to extreme heat, such as those that line the huge, electric-arc, melt-and-tilt ladles in steel plants. (Since you can't melt steel in a strictly steel cauldron, you need an intervening surface, a liner that varies in composition from the container's bottom to top—heavy on the magnesium mixture at the base, high in alumina up the sides, with an overarching dome of yet another type of brick. All of these compounds are variations on the basic aluminum silicate clay.)

Stoke-on-Trent

To get up to speed in the ceramics industry, Mano took a crash course in chemistry in Alexandria for admission to the British university at Stoke-on-Trent. Now under the name of Staffordshire University, the school has been at the center of the porcelain, tile, and bone china industry since 1914. (Among the signature "potteries" associated with the town are Wedgwood, Doulton, and Spode.)

Mano was assiduous in his studies, completing his curriculum in two, rather than the typical three years. But his fast-track finish was in jeopardy as finals loomed. He came down with the measles and faced the prospect of having to stay back for the next set of exams the following year. But Myrto came to the rescue, artfully applying the makeup needed to cover the spots, and he passed. (No word on whether his fellow students caught the measles.)

By this time, the company, KEREM, had closed its Egyptian facility and replicated it on the Greek coast near Elefsina. Mano became the plant manager and, drawing on the training he'd received in England, he suggested they might add a new product line—sanitary bathroom facilities. Though he wasn't able to bring the idea to fruition, Mano enjoyed his time with the company.

Ideal Standard

Again, through Myrto, Mano met a man who opened up a new pathway of opportunity in London through the export division of Ideal Standard (a European trademark of American Standard). Picking up on his continued interest in producing ceramics and sanitary ware, Mano wrote the company suggesting they might consider building a plant in Greece. Soon, the home office in New York sent a team to hear him out, and they were satisfied he'd made his case. Then the president of American Standard got involved, and an attempt was made to partner with KEREM in this venture with Mano as the go-between.

American Standard was asking for a 70 percent share of the new joint venture to be formed, a realistic offer, but KEREM declined. The linkup did not materialize. However, Standard was so impressed with Mano they told him, "If you stick with us, we'll go with you." And so they did, bringing him on board in 1962. Of course, Standard had no plant as of yet, and Mano continued at KEREM for a while, even as he quarterbacked the other developments, a process that took three years (involving, for example, legal clearance for foreign investment and the repatriation of funds to America).

At the outset, in 1965, there was a technical problem called "dunting," when the vitreous china would crack from the stress of firing and cooling. (Workers would hear an alarming "ping" as it gave way.) Since the glaze was something like a tire (or inner tube in days' past), when a fissure formed in its surface, the integrity of the whole was compromised. Fortunately, they learned how to reformulate the raw materials, and the dunting stopped. The result was a surge in their fortunes, with Ideal Standard surpassing its two Greek competitors on Mano's watch—a market position he maintained through 1979 when he moved to corporate headquarters in New York.

American Standard

American Standard had offered Mano other jobs through the years (a staff position in corporate strategy; a role at the Moser subsidiary), but those positions didn't appeal to him. He did accept the offer to become head of the international plumbing and export group, and it was a natural fit, not only because of his industry savvy, but also due to his mastery of a range of languages. (This had already served him well when, from his position in Greece, he used his Arabic to run Standard's exports to the Middle East.)

I once asked Mr. K what he thought of the competitors, and he called the roll. He named names, but I'll simply say he put them in their places on a scale of excellence. At the top end, he spoke of the fine qualities of one brand; at the other end, he marked down their tubs and basins over their willingness to countenance pin holes or slight deformations in the finished product and to pass along products that sagged or settled slightly in the process. And so, he made us writers aficionados of bathroom fixtures.

CHAPTER 3

"You'll Want to Talk to This Guy."
(American Standard's Turnaround)

In a 1994 article, *Fortune* magazine gave Mano credit for saving American Standard, and the piece began with his citing a Bible character.

> Emmanuel Kampouris, the Egyptian-born CEO of American Standard, studies the Bible not just for moral lessons, but for management guidance too. His idol is the redoubtable Nehemiah, who in 445 BC, rallied a small group of Israelites to rebuild the wall around Jerusalem in just 52 days. "It's an example of excellent leadership and smart management," marvels Kampouris. Inspired by the Old Testament, Kampouris is performing an epic feat on his own. In the past five years he has overcome the double scourge of huge debts and depressed markets to steer his company, a diversified manufacturer, from near ruin to robust health.[1]

Kelso

When Mano ascended to the top spot in 1990, he was less inclined to quote the Bible in interviews, but we'll wait until the next chapter to see how this changed. First, let's talk about the corporate turnaround.

The article goes on to explain, "American Standard's travails began in 1989 when tool manufacturer Black & Decker [hereafter, B&D] launched a hostile takeover bid. To rebuff the attack, Kelso & Co., a New York investment firm, engineered a leveraged buyout." Kelso acquired about 75 percent of the company, with employees holding the rest. What took place in a year was decades in the making.

The company had enjoyed its heyday in the 1920s, when it was a world leader in manufacturing radiators. (Several decades earlier, it had gotten a big boost when it was able to make good contacts with foreign buyers at the 1893 World's Fair in Chicago—the Columbian Exposition marking the 400th anniversary of Columbus's voyage to America). But the Great Depression meant a downward turn, and not even the post-World War II boom returned Standard to its original strength. So, in the 1960s, it tried diversifying to lift its fortunes, branching into enterprises from the construction of nuclear reactors and new homes to the manufacture of bank security devices.

Though there were bright spots here and there, it became clear the company had overreached drastically, and the aforementioned B&D came hunting. The challenge was enormous. Inventory was bloated and cash flow insufficient. Shares had fallen to around $35 when B&D offered $56 per share. To resist the takeover, Standard employed a "poison pill" defense involving the mass sale of new, discounted stock to its shareholders, thus diluting the value of its shares. Even so, it was still vulnerable to the highest bidder, which proved to be Kelso, which offered $78 a share. This was a "friendly takeover," in contrast with B&D's "hostile" try. They wanted to remove Standard from public trading, renew it, and return it to the market as the original company and at a profit—no small feat, given the circumstances.

Demand Flow Technology

To effect the turnaround, Emmanuel Kampouris was tapped to lead the corporation, in part because, in the initial interview, he spoke more about the virtues of American Standard's leaders around the world than about himself. Facing bankruptcy, the company sought loans to cover their indebtedness, but the offers were insufficient. Needing more cash, Mano charged his team to go find alternatives, and one of the members, Gary Biddle, said they needed to hear from John Costanza, who ran a consulting firm in Colorado. Meeting with the American Standard leadership on the twenty-first floor of their building in Manhattan, Costanza outlined Demand Flow Technology (DFT), which they adopted, and, soon, it multiplied the corporation's value, making it a model of efficiency and productivity. The corporation rewarded Mr. Kampouris for the dramatic turnaround, thus providing him with resources he would tap for Christian ministry through the Emmanuel Foundation. But, again, we get ahead of ourselves.

Costanza had argued the company could halve its inventory in a short time, freeing up $300 million in cash. The idea was to introduce a shorter manufacturing-cycle time, with mixed-model production and workers trained in more than one skill so they weren't stuck with assembling just one model. Instead, they could shift from one design to another and offer quick responses to orders as they arrived. Their work was tailored to immediate demand, and not to the steady generation of certain units in the hope demand would rise to draw down inventory generated by guesswork.

Within a month, they set up a pilot project in a Trane plant in Tyler, Texas, a residential-air conditioning factory acquired from General Electric. They provided the workers incentives for the transition and instituted an assembly cycle attuned to the flow of orders for specific products. It now took only an hour to produce what used to take half a day, and turnaround time for an order shrank from two weeks to eight hours.

With this encouraging result in hand, the company sent Costanza "on the road" to visit many of its 199 factories and lecture their leaders. They set up labs in every plant, offering workshops for the simulated production of two products—"Dynamo in the traditional way" and "Dynamo in the new way"—with the schooling completed in half a day. In this manner, they trained 22,000 people around the world in a single year. DFT, coupled with Total Quality Management (TQM), became the standard for American Standard.

To rejuvenate itself, the company also was pared down to four divisions, designated under the arcane language of the government's North American Industrial Classification System—American Standard ("Enameled Iron and Metal Sanitary Manufacturing" and "Plumbing Fixture Fitting & Trim Manufacturing"); Trane ("Air-conditioning & Warm Air Heating Equipment & Commercial & Industrial Refrigeration Equipment Manufacturing"); WABCO, from Westinghouse Air Brake Company ("Motor Vehicle Body Manufacturing"); and DiaSorin/Alimenterics ("Surgical & Medical Instrument Manufacturing").

By 1998, sales had reached $6.7 billion, and over the five-year span following its re-emergence as a public company, sales for American Standard grew annually at a double-digit rate. As the 1994 *Fortune* piece put it, "For this corporate Nehemiah, nothing is impossible."

Corporate Kudos

Business Week also praised the corporate turnaround, explaining how "Kampouris ... turned the $5 billion conglomerate into a growth machine." The effort, the magazine claimed, defied commonly-accepted business practices.

> Typical LBO [leveraged buyout] practice would have been to sell off its myriad businesses piecemeal. Although Kampouris sold off a few unwanted units, his real energy went into making the survivors better. Today, outsiders say Standard's success at finding gold in mundane commodes, coolers, and truck parts is an object lesson in smart manufacturing. Says management guru Michael Hammer: "They've learned how to take a manufacturing business and

run it like a bat out of hell" ... Investors are cheering: Since the IPO, Standard's stock has climbed 86% to around 37. "It's not hard to become a believer," says Kevin L. Risen, who co-manages two Neuberger & Berman Management Inc. mutual funds that own 3 million shares. "They are revolutionizing how products are delivered."[2]

Jack Welch, the acclaimed CEO of General Electric (which had sold American Standard the Tyler, Texas plant), has been a popular writer since his retirement and, in his book, *Winning*, he gives Mano (whom he calls "Manny") credit for his help.

GE was always trying to improve its working capital usage; we were always using too much, and increasing our inventory turns would help. But try as we might with all sorts of programs and tweaks, we just couldn't seem to get our annual turns above four.

In September 1994, Manny Kampouris was scheduled to speak at a dinner for the top thirty leaders in our company. At the time, Manny was the chairman and CEO of American Standard, the global plumbing and air-conditioning supply company and one of the largest customers of our motors business.

You couldn't help but notice that Manny wore a lapel pin emblazoned with the number "15" at its center. And soon enough, we all knew why.

For most of his talk that night, Manny regaled us with stories of how they had drastically improved inventory turns at American Standard ... Our team was awestruck. You could hear people thinking, if American Standard can improve inventory turns with its product mix and complicated manufacturing processes, why can't we? Before Manny could finish his talk, our business leaders were peppering him with question after question.

But that was just the beginning.

What followed was an avalanche of GE people visiting American Standard facilities, meeting with foremen and factory managers—all of them wearing lapel pins like Manny's. There was the occasional black sheep with a "10," but many more plant managers who wore pins boasting of twenty or twenty-five turns. We crawled all over their plants and picked their brains ...

The GE people who visited American Standard put what they had learned into practice in their own businesses. Over the next several years, these businesses adapted many of American Standard's processes to GE, and continually innovated and shared with each other. It worked. By 2000, GE's inventory turns had more than doubled, freeing up billions of dollars of cash.[3]

In his book on "getting things done," business consultant Ram Charan picks up the story:

Welch was excited by the idea, but he was not content to get just the concept—he wanted to understand the workings personally. Rather than sending some of his manufacturing people out to investigate it, he paid a visit to Kampouris and spent several hours with him.

Then he followed through to learn the hows at ground level. He accepted an invitation to speak at American Standard. During the dinner that followed, he sat between two of Kampouris's plant managers, one from Brazil and one from the U.K., whose plants had achieved annual inventory turns of 33 and 40 respectively. Welch spent the whole evening questioning them closely about the details—the tools, the social architecture, how they overcame resistance to the new methodology.

Did the chairman of GE have better things to do with his time? Absolutely not! ... By the time Welch retired in 2001, inventory turns had doubled, to 8.5.[4]

Integrity and Benevolence

While profits were essential to the survival (and flourishing) of the corporation and to the satisfaction of investors, corporate integrity was non-negotiable. Camille tells of the time when Mano made a verbal agreement on financing from First Boston. When an American Standard officer said he'd found another bank offering a better rate to the tune of a quarter of a percent (a not-insignificant dollar amount, given the size of the transaction), Mano refused to abandon First Boston, saying, "I gave them my handshake."

And this sort of integrity manifested itself in the work of his team. For instance, in the 1990s, American Standard was planning to build a factory in St. Petersburg, Russia, and they were two days away from signing the contract. Wilfried Delker, head of fittings worldwide, and his team were having breakfast when three Russian "gentlemen" walked in and asked, "May we join you?" They continued, "We've noticed you guys are going back and forth to Moscow. We want to offer protection for your goods and services in return for some payments." They'd been monitoring the team's every movement, and they knew everything they were doing. So instead of "playing ball," the Standard team "picked up their marbles and left," dropping Russia.

There were also problems in China. One fellow, "a bad apple," had bribed his way through to take over the factory and was, in effect, holding some foreign workers hostage. The central government proved less than helpful in this connection, so Standard executed an "amicable split" rather than continue with this arrangement.

Furthermore, the company sought to be a good neighbor wherever it went. In Bulgaria, they provided a local hospital with a heart-care unit. In Brazil, after noticing many of the workers had a gaunt look about them, they provided a regular, full breakfast at the factory. In the Philippines, they established a women's clinic, and when word came down that the plant manager was targeted for assassination, the women of the community came to his defense. In Egypt, the wife of a plant manager went to the city dumps to perform acts of charity.

Regard for the Blue Collar

Kampouris was known for his personal touch and keen attention to detail. American Standard board member and former U.S. Vice President Dan Quayle recalled a plant tour the two took together (again, quoting from *Business Week*): "He knew everybody. Not just the plant manager, he knew the foreman in the back shop, people in the front shop, he knew market and salespeople. He really has control." And this close attention to personnel gained him fresh recognition.

A 1999 *New York Times* article highlighted the emergence of "process teams," with less-exalted and more nebulous titles like "group leader" and "process owner" appearing on their business cards.[5] Indeed, his own CEO card simply listed him as "corporate leader." This shift was not particularly welcomed by "executives who saw the perks and prestige they felt had rewarded their hard work ... ripped away." Indeed, as Kampouris observed, "It ... meant learning to manage our egos, and accepting that we could learn as much from blue-collar workers as from each other." Again, it meant an "angst-filled cultural change. For managers, it [meant] the death of fancy titles, big offices, power over subordinates, all the ego trappings of corporate success."

This system also generated a host of "coaches" devoted to shepherding employees' careers. As Helmut Sander, who coached the coaches at the Brussels WABCO plant, said, "The process owners worry about customers, while the coaches worry about our people." Case in point:

> Diane Notta was an obscure finance department employee when her coach pushed her to brush up her customer-service skills and apply for the post she now holds shepherding customer orders at Trane. "This job would have seemed beyond my comfort zone if my coach hadn't led me through each step," Ms. Notta said.

By mid-1999, Standard had "278 people, many of whom once had fancy titles, [acting] as mentors to about 100 employees each." On this model, the "coaches catalogue their protégés' skills and interests, find them training to shore up weak spots and move them along fast enough to avoid boredom but slowly enough to prevent overload." This program led Cambridge, Massachusetts-based consultant Michael Hammer, who coined the term "re-engineering" and who designed "process organization," to observe American Standard was "more avant-garde than Silicon Valley companies that are long on promises of wealth but short on job flexibility and career counseling."

Of course, all of this is worth celebrating—the business acumen and success; the stewardship of natural resources in the provision of useful, quality products; the humanitarian efforts; the employment and nurture of many; the fealty to business ethics. But God was up to more than encouraging these things. He was also raising up and equipping Emmanuel Kampouris for extraordinary works of Christian ministry and philanthropy beyond the corporation.

All this being said, it's not surprising we teachers and students and pastors were a bit intimidated as we reported for work to a retired Fortune 500 CEO. After all, as Michael Hammer also noted, "Emmanuel Kampouris is mild mannered, he's courtly and delightful and kind. But if you're being halfhearted or insincere, you don't want to be on the receiving end of his evaluation." Still, we were all astonished at his patience, approachability, and yes, spirit of teamship, in our enterprise.

The Roast

One indication of his humility and forbearance was his apparent delight in the "roast" held at his 70th-birthday celebration in New York. It was an extraordinary evening at the Harmonie Club, a half-block from Central Park near the Plaza Hotel. We writers and our spouses were flown in from around America and the UK, and the Tommy Dorsey Orchestra provided the music. As grand as the event was, friends Karl Tiedemann and Eric Metaxas made sure it didn't get too stuffy. Karl had written the script, and Eric delivered the goods with PowerPoint accompaniment.

Here's the portion of that bogus bio devoted to Mano's corporate work:

> … Later, of course, he went into the business world, and eventually reached the summit as CEO of American Standard—a job that, in a sense, he'd been preparing himself for from a very young age. For virtually his entire life, except for a very brief period early on, Mano has been using bathrooms …

> Naturally, he didn't start out at the company as CEO. For a while he held the post called "Head of Worldwide Plumbing." But, he soon got tired of getting calls in the middle of the night from people in Nepal with clogged drains …

> When he did take control of American Standard, and its three divisions—plumbing products, air conditioning, and auto parts—he was determined

to impose a more efficient, up-to-date business model. Immediately, he sprang into action, shutting down the air conditioning outlets in Greenland and Antarctica ...

Mano has his own unique approach to corporate culture: He's said that he regards the Bible as the best guide ever to running a business. This has been positive in many ways—though it did cause some confusion at a 1993 sales meeting when he exhorted his staff to rise up and smite the Amorites, Hittites and Jebusites and drive them all from the land ... He later told the FBI that it was "merely a metaphor."

[B]eing a traditionalist, Mano didn't approve of casual Fridays. Under considerable pressure he did relent to the extent of allowing a casual quarter-hour every third Thursday ... of months that don't have an 'R' in them ...

Well, in any case, Mano's accomplishments at American Standard, how he turned that company around, is an amazing story. He took charge at a time of real crisis. It's said that the week he became CEO, a panhandler came up to him on the street and said, "Hey, man, spare some change? I'm broke," and Mano said, "Hey, pal, you think you got problems—I'm $3.2 billion in debt!" ...

He also took a hand in the company's air conditioning branch, the Trane company ... You probably know their clever little slogan: "It's hard to stop a Trane." Nice, huh? Well, that's thanks to Mano here. He insisted the company get rid of its disastrous early slogan: "Just step in front of a Trane." Saved many lives that way ... and several lawsuits ...

Efficiency is one of Mano's watchwords. He's always thinking in DFT terms. For instance, his name is actually Emmanuel, but he decided at an early age to be called Mano, enabling him to save more than two and a half years over the course of his life introducing himself ... That's why we're able to celebrate his 70th birthday, even though—in reality—he's only a little over sixty-seven ...

One of the highlights in Mano's life came just last year, when he finally became a U.S. citizen. That's right, you heard it here first—for all those years he was in charge of American Standard, Mano was not even an American! ... He was just another one of those shiftless foreigners who sneak into this country and create thousands of jobs ...

Now ... since Mano was the CEO of American Standard, many of you might be expecting a lot of stupid bathroom humor. Well, sorry that's not what we have on tap—we're not going to sink to that level. Mano is a dignified man, and when this evening is over, we want him to be flushed with pride ...

And, so, Mr. Emmanuel Kampouris, distinguished CEO, endured— and even enjoyed—one hundred forty people laughing at his expense.

CHAPTER 4

An Invitation to Times Square Church
(An Awakening Out of Grief)

In 1992, when Mano was fifty-five, he lost Myrto, his beloved wife of thirty-two years. She had succumbed to breast cancer at age fifty-two. His grief was profound and visible, and he occasionally excused himself from corporate executive meetings as he found himself tearing up.

In the midst of this season, Joe Schuchert, head of the Kelso group, invited Mano to attend Times Square Church with him. (When some in the leadership at American Standard wondered out loud whether their grieving CEO was up to the task, Schuchert, a strong Christian, assured them that, given time, Mano would level out emotionally and that, in the meantime, he was perfectly able to lead.)

At the church, Mano heard founding pastor David Wilkerson, author of *The Cross and the Switchblade*, preach with arresting passion. Mano's own worship disposition was Anglican, but Wilkerson struck a chord with him. It was his first exposure to this sort of preaching, marked by such a spirit of authority and sincerity. He was much impressed. (At the time, he didn't suspect it would one day help inspire and inform an online publication called *Kairos Journal*, but the imprint of those messages remained.)

Christianity Today called Wilkerson the "wooden-tongued preacher," albeit while they were reporting on the power of his work.[6] As his son observed, regarding the strong response to "altar calls" given at the end of his sermons, "Those powerful moments were not the effect of my dad's oratorical skills, because he basically read his sermons from his script." As another explained, "He was like some of the old revivalists. There was so much prayer behind his sermons that there was a powerful anointing on the reading, and people were converted."

A Call to Anguish

One of David Wilkerson's most notable sermons was *A Call to Anguish*, preached in September 2002. Here are excerpts (and they're not at all "wooden tongued"):[7]

> I look at the whole religious scene today, and all I see are the inventions and ministries of man and flesh. It's mostly powerless. It has no impact on the world. And I see more of the world coming into the church and impacting the church rather than the church impacting the world …

> I see the music taking over the house of God. I see entertainment taking over the house of God. An obsession with entertainment in God's house, a hatred of correction and a hatred of reproof. Nobody wants to hear it anymore … Whatever happened to anguish in the house of God? Whatever happened to anguish in the ministry? It's a word you don't hear in this pampered age. You don't hear it. Anguish means extreme pain and distress. The emotions so stirred that it becomes painful. Acute, deeply felt inner pain because of conditions about you, in you, or around you … Agony of God's heart. We've held onto our religious rhetoric and our revival talk, but we've become so passive …

You search the Scripture, and you'll find that when God determined to recover a ruined situation, he would seek out a praying man and he would take him down into the waters of anguish. He would share his own anguish, for what God saw happening to his church and to his people …

You find it in the book of Nehemiah. Jerusalem is in ruins … How is God going to deal with this? How is God going to restore the ruin? … Folks, look at me. Nehemiah was not a preacher, he was a career man … This was a praying man. God found a man who would not just have a flash of emotion, not just some great sudden burst of concern and then let it die. He said, "No. I broke down and I wept and I mourned and I fasted. Then I began to pray night and day" …

Does it matter to you today, does it matter to you at all that God's spiritual Jerusalem, the Church, is now married to the world? … Closer than that, does it matter about the Jerusalem that's in our own hearts? The sign of ruin that is slowly draining spiritual power and passion …

There is a great difference between anguish and concern … Concern is something that begins to interest you … Where are the Sunday School teachers that weep over kids they know are not hearing and are going to hell? …

There's nothing of the flesh will give you joy. I don't care how much money, I don't care what kind of new house, there is absolutely nothing physical that can give you joy. It is only what is accomplished by the Holy Spirit when you obey him and take on his heart ...

Build the walls around your family. Build the walls around your own heart ...

Mount Athos

As Mano continued to attend Times Square Church and join in after-church brunches at the Schuchert's, a spiritual awakening occurred. It had begun during a time of prayer at Mount Athos, which he'd visited on a number of occasions. It was there he had prayed for the balance of three days and began to experience the transformation of his heart, of his spiritual orientation. Reflecting on those days, Mano observed that he'd not before met men so detached from society's affairs, yet they also considered their work strategic, in that they believed their prayers helped sustain the world. Mano would stand beside the monks as they prostrated themselves in prayer, and though, as he recounts, he didn't have a vision of Christ, he sensed the love of Jesus in those moments.

I should note that access to Mount Athos and those monasteries is not a simple thing, something to plan as a stop on one's European tour. You need special permission from both state and religious authorities, and only men may apply. (Charles Marnham, whom we'll meet later in the book, once spent time on Athos, accompanying a Greek architect, whose job it was to evaluate the upkeep of those ancient buildings. For this, they had to gain clearance from the Patriarch of Constantinople, the highest-ranking leader in the Eastern Orthodox Church.)

Bob Phillips

Another one of the Times Square Church pastors, Bob Phillips, was helpful in those days. He was a Kentucky native who attended the Southern Baptist Theological Seminary (SBTS) in Louisville, where

I now teach. He was an itinerant Bible preacher and teacher based in Bedford, Texas, when David Wilkerson established an East Texas center for World Challenge, an outworking of his Teen Challenge ministry, launched in New York City in 1958. The center sat on the 365-acre Twin Oaks Ranch, land that Wilkerson later sold for ten cents on the dollar to Youth with a Mission (YWAM)—essentially giving it to them when he sensed this was God's pleasure. (While there, Wilkerson influenced Christian musicians Keith Green, Dallas Holmes, and 2nd Chapter of Acts.)

One day, Wilkerson overheard a sermon tape his house painter was playing. The message was by somebody named Bob Phillips. Impressed, Wilkerson reached out to Bob, and they met in Tyler, Texas. As Bob recalled:

> We spent three days together at the Ramada Inn in Tyler going through the Scriptures. There's a passage in Ezekiel 44 that's a pretty hard one. It talks about God's people breaking covenant with him [and of God's allowing his preachers to feed the congregation the false message they desired]. I'd been preaching from that chapter in a lot of my messages, and David wanted me to share my insights with him … He just fell over. He curled up in a fetal position and began to weep and weep and weep. He was feeling the consequence of that passage of Scripture, and he was crying for the nation. As I looked at David, I was still upright. All I could think was, "I've been preaching this message for a while, but it has never affected me the way it's affecting this man right now." I remember having this thought: "He's feeling what God feels—and I want that." I saw a man who not only carried the burden of God but was deeply impacted by it. That was David's tenderness. He was thinking and feeling with God's heart.[8]

When Wilkerson returned to New York in 1987 to establish Times Square Church, he invited Bob to join him to help him get started.

Before finding a permanent home for the church, the congregation met in a variety of places, including an outdoor venue, Bryant Park, behind the New York Public Library. It was there one evening that a demon-possessed man disrupted the meeting. He was trying to bite people and tear up the hedges. Bob went over to calm him down, but the man yelled, "Tell 'em to get back!" He dashed across the street, circled a light pole, and then ran back to the park and threw himself into the bushes. As the Lord delivered him and returned him to his right mind, the man exclaimed, "Thank you, Jesus," and began hugging people.

After the service, as Bob was walking away from the park with David and his wife, Gwen, Wilkerson asked him to consider joining him as a church planter in New York. And Bob did. He and his wife Sherri moved to the city and got in on the ground floor of one of America's most remarkable churches.

A Church Home on Broadway

They began in a place called Town Hall and got bumped around now and then. They tried to buy a theater at 8th Avenue and 42nd Street near the Port Authority Bus Terminal, but that didn't materialize. Then, in 1989, they were able to lease the Mark Hellinger Theater (where the original production of *My Fair Lady* ran from 1956 to 1962 and *Jesus Christ Superstar* was performed more than seven hundred times in the early 1970s). But the theater had fallen on hard times, hitting bottom when the show, *Legs Diamond*, lasted only a month. The Nederlander Organization, which owned the theater, was ready to sell it at a reduced price ($16 million), even leaving the sound system intact. The church agreed to buy it in 1991 with financial help from Kelso's Joe Schuchert. (Negotiations had to be kept quiet because of "Mark Hellinger's status in the arts community. If the media got wind of a pending deal, there would be an outcry from the theater circles and the deal would never go through.")[9]

Convinced they had found God's provision, the church later turned down a lucrative offer for the space when Broadway's fortunes improved. After enjoying a strong run in London, the producers of *Miss Saigon* approached them. As Bob Phillips recalls:

> They made an offer of about ten million dollars more than we paid for it. Of course, it wasn't for sale. They even offered David the theater across the street, but he didn't do that either. That said a lot to me. David's concern was not money; he was concerned about the purpose God had sent him there for. That was paramount to him.[10]

David's son Gary had observed the same spirit in his father.

> Dad once disclosed to a friend the philosophy he had formed about money. "God will allow millions of dollars to flow through your hands if you will not close your fists around it. If you allow it to flow through your hands, God will use it for the cause of his kingdom …
>
> During the first Sunday service at the Mark Hellinger, Dad made a point in his opening announcement. "There are no superstars here," he said. "There is only the Bright and Morning Star" …
>
> It was one of the biggest stages on Broadway," Uncle Don [David Wilkerson's brother] says. "And there was no hype, only worship and God's Word."[11]

So, with this focus, the church prospered, with attendees coming from New Jersey and Pennsylvania (a "two-tape drive," i.e., a trip long enough to listen to two cassettes).

Mark Coppenger

"Pastor Bob"

Bob Phillips (whom the Kairos group often called "Pastor Bob") was no slack preacher, either. And he could be particularly pointed when addressing the sins of the church and the clergy.

> I've heard preachers quote the verse, "If we are faithless, He remains faithful: for He cannot deny Himself" (2 Timothy 2:13). They then justify: "If you should sin, just confess your sin. God is faithful; He understands." They say this as if compromise is a pattern or option for Christian living: "Sin, then confess; sin, then confess," and on and on. We call it "carnal Christian living." God calls it an abomination!

> Such anemic preaching is one of the most serious lies proclaimed from the pulpit today. It has turned out a degenerated form of Christianity that merely gives God lip service, but never the heart. Multitudes of people today think that merely to say, "Forgive me," and then to go on sinning will get them into heaven.[12]

As blunt as he could preach, Bob also helped Wilkerson to temper his prophetic edge with tenderness. Gary Wilkerson puts it this way:

> Dad had remained fixated on the subject of covenant since his first encounter with Bob in Tyler. Dad's initial focus had been on the judgment aspects of God's covenant with man. Now, through his continued reading of the Puritans and others, Dad had slowly turned his gaze to the beneficial aspects.

> The implications of covenant grace challenged his very moorings. He saw plainly that his prior notion

of grace had been rooted in trying to please the Father by obeying his laws, doing more, occupying himself with responsibilities. My dad had never turned away from a single truth revealed in God's Word—especially if that truth convicted him—but now he was hesitant. He feared that a headlong dive into pure grace might make him relax, pulling him away from his passion for God.

Yet he knew there was nowhere to go other than forward. ... I was proud of how Dad attacked the subject. I remember seeing a stack of volumes by John Owen on the desk in his study ...

What I saw happen with Dad was an evolution from the ministry of condemnation to the ministry of reconciliation. He received letters from people whose lives were being changed by his messages on covenant grace. For years they had been shackled by guilt, laboring under a performance-driven faith, but now they wrote saying, "Thank you, I've been set free!" Other longtime newsletter readers had an opposite reaction, writing, "Are you getting soft? It's been awhile since you've given a correction or a rebuke. What happened to the preacher of 'no compromise'?"

The changes taking place in my father registered on deeper and deeper levels. At one point he was compelled to call fifteen people he had been estranged from and ask them to forgive him. There were people whose relationships with Dad had ended badly, some of them his fault and some of them not. Regardless, he owned up to his part in the breach and sought reconciliation in a spirit of love.

> Several of the people he called wept. This was something they had hoped for over the years. Now Dad was able to catch up on their lives, asking if they were still in ministry, inquiring how he might help them. Doing this gave my father a peace he had never known.[13]

Pastor Bob's heart for God also blessed Mano. Bob would go to Mano's office in the Grace Building on 6th Avenue or to one of the clubs Mano belonged to, and they would talk about Mano's wife, Myrto. The conversation would move to biblical matters as Mano "made inquiries about the Lord." Sometimes, he would bring up a story he'd read in the Bible, and Bob would explain it.

Bob recalled that when Mano first came to Times Square, he was a cultural/devotional Christian with a hunger for God, which he'd had even as a child. But Myrto's death and his grief produced in him a fresh and deep seriousness about his spiritual condition. And so, he moved gradually into a confessing evangelical faith. The transition was evident to all.

Mano, the polo player in Egypt

Mano (front row, center) on the King's School fencing team (Photo by King's School.)

Emmanuel Kampouris (front row, left) with members of the Combined Cadet Force, King's School, Bruton, Somerset, 1952 (Photo by King's School.)

Newly wed Myrto and Emmanuel Kampouris

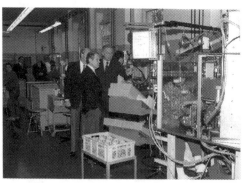

Mano touring WABCO plant in Hanover, Germany

Mano with Orthodox priests at 10th century Monastery
Xiropotamos, Mount Athos, Greece

Mano with sons, Andrew and Alexander, and the 44th U.S. Vice President, Dan Quayle

CAMILLE

CHAPTER 5

"Who's That Girl with the Voice?" (Onto the Stage)

Mano confided in Bob that he didn't think he'd ever marry again, nor was he interested. But God had other plans, and so we begin another thread in this narrative.

Camille Bonora was the daughter of an Italian-American father, himself born in the U.S., and an Italian-born mother. He studied law at Georgetown, and, when Camille was three, the Bonoras returned to Rome for five years. There, she enjoyed "early childhood education" at the Marymount International School. Back in America and living on Capitol Hill in Washington, she attended the all-girl Immaculata High School, which later closed when the property sold to American University.

One day in church, two nuns were particularly impressed with the strong voice they heard singing behind them. It belonged to ten-year-old Camille, and word of this prodigy soon found its way to Sister Jacqueline, the music director at St. Cecelia's. Once discovered, Camille was tapped for musical performances, including the role of the crippled boy, Amahl, in Gian Carlo Menotti's *Amahl and the Night Visitors* (the "night visitors" being the wise men, or *magi*, in search of the baby Jesus). Though, in his production notes, Menotti wrote, "It is the express wish of the composer that the role of Amahl should always be performed by a boy," they cut Camille's hair and gave her a crutch, and she was good to go.

Gonzaga College High School was for boys only, but they needed an Eliza Doolittle for their production of *My Fair Lady* and turned to Camille. Years later, she reflected on the part, concluding she'd found her Henry Higgins in Emmanuel Kampouris, whose demeanor was Britishly-refined, down to the way in which he cut his sandwiches. (She also recalled the Lord's healing of Amahl, a parallel to her subsequent spiritual healing in Manhattan.)

In Washington, DC, Camille attended Catholic University of America, and her studies ranged throughout the liberal arts, with coursework in Chaucer and Shakespeare. She earned Phi Beta Kappa honors for her efforts, and she took a degree in voice, majoring in opera. She performed her senior recital in three languages—Italian, French, and English.

Culturally, she had every encouragement to press on in the performing arts. Ethnic Italians and their artistic deliverances were everywhere. A fair listing would be staggeringly long and would include everyone from Fellini and Coppola to DeNiro and DeVito, from Caruso and Pavarotti to DeLuise and Leno ... and, yes, Menotti, who set the stage for Camille's role as Amahl.

Operatic music played freely in the Bonora home, and her parents took her often to a variety of productions, including the comic ballet, *Coppelia*, in which a young man is smitten by a lifelike doll on a balcony—one he mistakes for a girl. She vividly remembers her first exposure to a musical *Annie, Get Your Gun* at the National Theater, with Ethel Merman belting out songs in the lead. (Camille later did a tribute to Merman on *Sesame Street*.)

Though she initially set her sights on music performance, she didn't (in her words) have a "career voice." And Broadway stars (notwithstanding the 5'3" Bernadette Peters, who was a powerful stage presence in the day) are also typically taller than Camille's 5'2" build. So, she found her opening niche doing Civil War-themed shows for tourists at Ford's Theater, site of President's Lincoln's assassination.

In God's providence, a lighting technician from New York had come to DC to work with a show at Ford's and had rented an apartment there for three months, leaving his New York apartment free. He offered it to Camille for a month, and her brother pushed her to take it. She'd been out of college for a year, serving as a receptionist at a law firm in addition to her theater work. So off she went with two suitcases, knowing no one up there, bound for a roach-infested, studio apartment on the Upper West Side. Before long, she found better accommodations and took root in the city. The job she landed as a singing waitress in a short-order establishment wasn't all she wanted, but it was a start.

A friend from DC, Brenda Bass, a trumpet player in music school who also worked in a comedy club, came up to help her settle in. Brenda had befriended comedian Larry Miller, and he was pleased to hear she was in the Big Apple. They decided to meet, and both brought along friends—she, Camille and he, Jerry Seinfeld. So, three days into her New York sojourn, Camille met Jerry. This was the late seventies, before 'Seinfeld' was a household word, and she asked him what he did. (She wasn't that familiar with "standup," since cable specials and ubiquitous comedy clubs were not yet the order of the day.)

At the time, Jerry had a girlfriend, but their relationship didn't last through the fall. For one thing, he was somewhat taken by Camille, and in the late 1979 holiday season, Jerry asked Larry, "What happened to that Italian girl?" Larry had trouble tracking her down; his contact, Brenda, had gone on tour, and he had to wait for her return to get a fix on Camille. But he succeeded, and Jerry started dating her in December.

When she went to see him perform, she found him "clean and good" and artful in handling a heckler. (Neither Jerry nor Larry "worked blue," trading in off-color humor or stooping to obscenity.) The relationship budded and continued for months, even including a visit to her home in Washington. They made something of an odd couple, she a "lapsed Roman Catholic," he an ethnic Jew dabbling in

Scientology. But it was working … until June 1980, when Jerry moved to Los Angeles to begin his work in television. (His first of many *Tonight Show* appearances came in May of 1981, and the eponymous sit-com *Seinfeld*, which ran for ten years, began in 1989.)

The goodbye was tearful, and the break was not abrupt, for he flew her out there once for a visit. But a bigger change was taking place, a spiritual one, and Jerry played a role in that as well (though it would make their future as a couple impossible). It started when he told Camille that she was so funny that she should be on the comedy stage, and he recommended a class she might take.

CHAPTER 6

"Here, Read This." (Finding the Lord in Manhattan)

At Jerry Seinfeld's prompting, Camille enrolled in an improvisational comedy class, one where she met Karl Tiedemann, a man who helped lead her to the Lord. Seinfeld had commended the course to Karl as well, and so, in God's providence, they got acquainted there.

Karl was the son of a Columbia University professor. He'd been interested in comedy since the age of nine or ten and, by the late 1970s, was exploring the possibilities in standup. He frequented the Comic Strip Live, where Seinfeld was a regular emcee. One evening, Jerry put in a good word for a place that taught "theme work" in comedy. Karl asked him about it, and Jerry pointed him to the very course to which he'd steered Camille.

Karl was a Christian, as was another student, Suzanne Smart. They befriended Camille and, as their relationship with her grew, began to witness to their faith. Karl gave her some literature. She remembers particularly C. S. Lewis's *Mere Christianity*; he recalls Catherine Marshall's *Adventures in Prayer*. Sometimes, the three of them met for lunch, where talk often turned to the Lord. Then there were the Bible studies at Calvary Baptist Church (across from Carnegie Hall), where Karl was a member.

In those days, when Donald Hubbard was pastor, a small group of show-biz people connected to the church met daily for prayer and

Bible study. Camille attended sometimes, and she was particularly struck by Psalm 37:4: "If you delight in the Lord, he'll give you the desires of your heart." As Karl remembers, she was not resistant to the faith, but rather quite eager to learn more. So it was that she came to "pray the sinner's prayer" (her testimony, employing the familiar expression) and receive Christ as Savior and Lord in the fall of 1980.

As for comedy, Camille was getting some work and some laughs, and, indeed, was getting good at this new art form. One day, her teacher told her that someone had become ill, and she wondered if Camille could go on in her place. It was a nice affirmation.

As Camille, Karl, and Suzanne advanced in their studies, they decided to form a troupe and call themselves "Laffing Matters." They were joined by Bob and Christine Calvo and Sterling Swan, and they began to perform a combination of improv and sketch comedy. Though they made club appearances, their main work was for private parties and corporate events, where they enjoyed some success over the two years the group existed. (Karl went on to write for *Late Night with David Letterman* and introduced the host to the redoubtable Calvert DeForest, who appeared regularly as Larry "Bud" Melman; Camille appeared in a Letterman sketch with Melman, with both getting pies in the face at the end.)[14]

Camille's told us some improv troupes operate with a totally free-flowing style, but for her class, there were strict rules even though the results might look free-form. One of the rules was that you had seconds to establish the scene, to tell the other person what's happening, and the more specific you could be the better. For example, you're in a doctor's office, and you open with the words, "Dad, you've come here three times this week as my patient." And then your partner has to run with it and not negate what you said. So, "I'm not your dad. I'm your husband," was out of bounds; it would wreck the whole enterprise.

Tribute to Vaudeville

One of their sketches was a tribute to Vaudeville where Karl approached a librarian (Camille), requesting a library card. She said that would be fine, but he'd first need to answer some questions. The exchanges were rim-shot quick:

> Any children?
> Three, a boy and girl.
> A boy and a girl? What's the third one?
> It's so young, who can tell.
>
> Are you looking at my legs?
> No. I'm above that.
>
> Did any of your family ever suffer from insanity?
> No. They all rather seemed to enjoy it.
>
> How about your father? How'd you get along with him?
> One day, he took me down to the lake and threw me in.
> What's wrong with that?
> Everyone else was skating on it. But I decided not to let a traumatic childhood stand in my way.
> Spoken like a man.
> Yes, I do impressions.
>
> Do you have any hobbies?
> Yes, hunting.
> Hunting! Why do you go around shooting dumb animals?
> The smart ones all hide.
>
> (Offered a chair since he wasn't feeling well, he sits.)
> Are you comfortable?
> I make a good living.

What do you do?

Nothing. Anyway, I don't have to get a job. I inherited money from my uncle when he died.

Oh, were you sorry to see him go?

Not really. He was a mean man. He used to get hate mail from Quakers.

I have an uncle like that. He runs a furniture factory, and the other day he fell into an upholstering machine.

How is he now?

Completely recovered.

Then Karl starts asking the questions:

Tell me, what's your name?

My name is Mary Jackson, PhD, LLD, BA, MA, MS, MD.

You mean ...?

That's right; my last name is Phdlldbamamsmd.

Well, that's a novelty. What about your education? How far did you go in school?

Well, if I liked the boy, I let him kiss me.

No, no. I mean, did you go to college or did ...

I graduated from high school.

Oh, *cum laude*?

(Camille, yelling) I SAY, I GRADUATED FROM HIGH SCHOOL!

I see. Were you a good student?

I did very well in foreign languages.

Oh ... *Sprechen zie Deutsch*?

Oui, Oui.

Well, I must be going now ...

Oh, and I also have to find a birthday present for my brother, and it's very hard.

Really?
Yes. Maybe you can help me. What would you rec-
ommend for the man who has everything?
Penicillin.

The Ultimate Improvisation

Another sketch played off the familiar improv drill of starting a scene
with a suggestion from the audience.

> To begin with, as always, we have to come to you,
> the audience, for your input. So, to get us started,
> could you give us the suggestion of a carcinogenic
> unicellular amoeba? (pause) Any at all? There's lots
> of them. Just shout them out.

> (Troupe member #2 rushes in to save the situation.)
> Excuse me, honey ... I'm sorry, I think you might be
> getting just a little bit overambitious ... Why don't
> you just let me handle it.

> (to the audience) I'm sorry, she gets a little carried
> away at times, but it is true that we do need your help
> to get started ... So, to get us underway, could you
> give us the suggestion of any one of the cuneiform
> characters common to all three languages on the
> Rosetta Stone? (pause) Just one?

> (Troupe member #3 dashes in to save the situation.)
> Uh, I think you may have started off on the wrong
> foot; why don't you let me take over? (to the audi-
> ence) Okay, I'm sorry. We would like to get this scene
> rolling, so could you please give us a suggestion? Just
> shout it out, any one of the legal precedents cited in
> the Sacco-Vanzetti trial.

(No answer, and his/her affability turns into disgust). Okay … maybe it's OUR fault. Maybe we've just been aiming a bit too high for you … All right … Could you give us the suggestion of a PRIMARY COLOR? (Exasperated) Red. Thank you. How about a fruit? Thank you, sir. A banana. A day of the week? Great. Tuesday.

Red. Banana. Tuesday. (And the scene begins):
1st Player: Hi. It's *Tuesday.*
2nd Player: Boy, is my face *red.*
3rd Player: Hey, want to share my lunch? Have a *banana.*
(They walk off dejectedly, as failed artists.)

Tribute to Opera

And then there was the *Tribute to Opera*, where Karl narrated, and Camille sang, with piano accompaniment. Working from their sketch notes, we find:

The time is the fourteenth century; the place, the heart of the Holy Roman Empire. (Camille sings a striking phrase or two.) Beautiful, isn't it? And it kills any flying insect within fifty feet … Last night she went two notes higher—had the place full of dogs …

Lucinda is the burgermeister's daughter, a gay, radiant girl (Camille trills.) … She is dying of consumption … (Camille coughs, wheezes, retches, etc.) and indeed has been dying of consumption for the past seventeen years … By this time her family suspects that it's her idea of a joke … Still, she is her father's pride and joy, which indicates that he hasn't much of either.

(Camille picks up the narration as Karl puts on a sash.) The family's fate is to be intertwined with that of Rudolfo, a young soldier quartered at the inn of Ubaldo. A brave and gallant warrior, Rudolfo does not know the meaning of the word 'fear' … He also doesn't know the meaning of the words 'cat' and 'saucer' and 'lampshade' …

Lucinda (Camille) falls madly in love with him, but they are separated when he is called up to serve four consecutive decades in the Hundred Years War.

(Karl picks up the narration.) Years later, Lucinda has fallen upon hard times. She is now a common, dirty laborer, working in a sweatshop, packaging buttered toast for wealthy landowners. And she sings a pathetic song of lament, *Ponte, Pone, Pianomo* ("I Am Mocked by Fate and Receive No Overtime").

But suddenly, she takes hold of herself. She shakes off her despair, and, in a stirring aria, resolves to face the future, whatever it may bring (singing, "*Domani, Domani,*" Italian for "Tomorrow, Tomorrow," which was popular in the musical *Annie*, then on Broadway).

(The pianist picks up the narration as Camille dissolves into a coughing fit.) Suddenly Rudolfo starts in amazement … That cough! Where had he heard it before? … Could it be? Could it possibly be his beloved Lucinda? … Could this dirty grubby little creature drooling and babbling to herself possibly be the girl he loves? … Yes! … It *is* Lucinda … Suddenly, Rudolfo is filled with compassion … Love overrides concern for his personal hygiene, and they embrace.

(The pianist continues.) All's well that ends well; the two lovers are reunited, Lucinda has regained her health, and Rudolfo still has one good ear left (the other one wrecked by one of Lucinda's lovely high notes). Joy and happiness abound. So Lucinda does the only thing she can think of to properly end the opera … She takes out a knife and kills herself. (Camille falls to ground.) And now Lucinda must sing the endless aria: *Pericloso mi dia demoto* ("Stand back, Everyone—I'm Gonna Die Now").

Bible Study with Cigarette in Hand

Now let's move from the sublimely ridiculous back to the sublimely spiritual.

Keen to study the Bible as a new Christian, Camille would rise at 10:00 a.m. (having performed and/or waitressed late into the previous evening, and then cleaned the cappuccino machine). After breakfast, she'd sit down for three hours of Bible study, cigarette in hand. Her boss at Ichabod's (a bar/restaurant at 77th Street and 2nd Avenue), Gianni "John" Valenti, would let her off from time to time for "gigs" or for Bible studies, but he was skeptical, especially when she asked him to release her from helping with Sunday brunch to attend church. He was finally able to get a take on her Christianity and her legitimacy as an entertainer when he came to some of her shows. (In 1996, Valenti reopened the Birdland club, which Charlie Parker had dubbed "the jazz corner of the world," on West 44th; Maynard Ferguson, a trumpet favorite of mine through my college years, "christened" the event with a performance.)

Camille recalls Valenti's tough exterior ("Everybody was afraid of him"). He'd say she was one of his worst waitresses and he should fire her, but then added, "Who would hire you?" So, he'd keep her on. In fact, he was a "godsend" who "did hundreds of favors for her" in the four-plus years she worked there. For one thing, he'd cut her a lot of slack to accommodate her performance schedule. For another, he'd help her, the "starving artist," with food; she'd ask and get permission to take home the remainder of a quart of milk or some bread left over.

It was at the restaurant that Camille met Patti Booth, who later became a travel agent and served us on the Kairos writing team. She and Camille were the "goodie two-shoes" of the restaurant, the "pure" ones who didn't do cocaine or go home with the customers. In fact, Valenti came to call her "The Madonna" (playing off the stage name of a fast-rising pop star of the day) and accepted her counsel on such matters as making sure his mother had a Perugina Egg at Easter, an Italian tradition. (The factory in Perugia, Italy, makes fifty thousand eggs a day, puts a surprise inside each one, and ships them around the world.) Indeed, she went down to Little Italy to get him one so he wouldn't disappoint his mother.

So this was the setting in which Camille began her new walk as a Christian, a season in which she became involved in an artists' Bible study in the theater district, a group that met between matinees and evening performances. The 5:00 to 7:30 p.m. slot gave them time to assemble, and the group swelled to a hundred. Eventually, it became a church, full of singers and dancers, calling itself the Unbroken Chain.

Funny You Never Knew

I should note that Camille counts comedy a "gift from God." She says it's a fearful thing to step out on stage and perform for a demanding audience, relying upon your wits, in improv, to come up with the next line—a lot of pressure. But she found her new walk with Christ freed her up for better work. Offstage before her entry, to fortify herself, she would repeat, "Where the Spirit of the Lord is, there is freedom" (2 Corinthians 3:17) and "Perfect love casts out fear" (1 John 4:18).

Recently, after thirty years, the Lord reunited her with Karl Tiedemann (along with New Zealand film maker Andrew Hunt) to produce *Funny You Never Knew*, a celebration of the careers of classic, 1950s comedians, Imogen Coca (who starred opposite Sid Caesar in *Your Show of Shows*), Martha Raye (who was awarded an Oscar and the Presidential Medal of Freedom for her decades of USO service, from World War II to Vietnam), and George Gobel (whose eponymous television show featured such guests as Jimmy Stewart, Henry Fonda, and Shirley MacLaine). These greats are seen through the eyes of Fred Willard (who starred in such "mockumentaries" as *This is Spinal Tap, Best in Show, Waiting for Guffman*, and *A Mighty Wind*) and Kevin Pollak (whose comedy specials have aired on HBO and Showtime.)

Unbroken Chain

One of the Bible teachers in this new church was Ben Harney, who won a 1982 Tony Award for Leading Actor in a Musical. The show was *Dreamgirls*, in which his character was modeled on Motown producer Barry Gordy. Harney was a graduate of Manhattan's High School for Music and Arts (now named for the Mayor who founded it, Fiorello LaGuardia), a school which counts among its alumni such luminaries as Al Pacino, Jennifer Aniston, Billy Dee Williams, Bela Fleck, Pinchas Zuckerman, and Steven Bochco. (Years later, in the early 2000s, Harney teamed with Camille to produce the five-part Christian video series for children, *Ben and Eddie*, with funding from Joe Schuchert, who'd first invited Mano to Times Square Church.)

Unbroken Chain was a predominately black, Holiness church, pastored by Maria DeLites (her real name). The services were electric and theatric. The singing centered on worship songs and, throughout, many of the congregants expressed themselves with abandon. It was gratifying and exhilarating for a young Christian, and Camille attended for five years.

There was great emphasis on personal holiness and spiritual discipline, bathed in Bible study and prayer. "Come out and be separate" (2 Corinthians 2:17) was a church watchword, and Camille had the strong sense that if she gave up her consecration, she would be like Samson who lost his hair; she'd lose her freedom and skill at comedy. Looking back, she likens herself to a Marine or to one preparing for the Olympics, with a regimen which got her into bed by 11:00 p.m., a regimen she came to value even more when, years later, she had to be on the Sesame Street set by 8:30 a.m. (a gig I'll soon explain) and up for an hour of Bible study first thing in the morning.

As edifying as her years at Unbroken Chain proved to be, Camille sensed she needed a "change in diet." The sermons were repetitive, and many of her friends were now attending Times Square Church, where David Wilkerson was pastor. It, too, was a church with a sampling of celebrities, including John Thompson (who co-wrote *El Shaddai* with Michael Card) and Patti Roberts (the first wife of Richard Roberts, Oral Roberts's son).

Times Square Church

At Times Square, Camille met Bob Phillips, who later played a major role in her joint ministry with Mano. He was one of three pastors, along with David Wilkerson and his brother, Don. Bob preached at most of the morning services; David preferred Sunday evening; and Don spoke at the Tuesday evening meetings. Bob also went out with some of the attendees to the Stage Deli on 7th Avenue and counseled artists such as Dianne Venora, a rising star, who'd appeared as Charlie Parker's wife in Clint Eastwood's biopic, *Bird*, and who'd later play Al Pacino's wife in *Heat*. As with most Christians in the theater, Venora struggled with whether or not she should take on certain roles (a tension Camille experienced even on *Sesame Street* from time to time).

CHAPTER 7

"Would You Do Voiceover?" (On to the Muppets)

When I told Camille the chapters of this book would turn upon "divine appointments," she noted there was a complementary reality—that there were "divine non-appointments," if you will. For instance, she wanted to be on *Saturday Night Live* and was pleased to help with a tryout sketch where she got laughs for her performance. But they didn't pick her, and so it was back to waitressing, to "waiting on God." The lesson proved edifying, for she was learning to "embrace different seasons" and to "be content."

She learned to embrace the spirit of Moses' request in Exodus 33:15. When God told him to lead the liberated Hebrews to the Promised Land, Moses replied, "If your Presence does not go with us, do not send us up from here." He didn't want to get out ahead of God, and neither did this Manhattan waitress. Rather, she abided in her favorite verse, Psalm 37:4: "Take delight in the Lord, and he will give you the desires of your heart."

Of course, "waiting on God" didn't mean "doing nothing," and Camille was performing her due diligence in the field, contacting potential agents. One came asking whether she'd be interested in voiceover work, and she signed on. Before long, she met a customer at the restaurant who also did voiceovers. He started dating a girl who worked with the Muppets and helped steer Camille in that direction.

She'd given him a tape, which caught the attention of the Muppets folks, and soon an audition call came from Jim Henson.

Jim Henson and Meryl Sheep

She thought they were merely selling a workshop, since she had no experience with puppets. Besides, though she was familiar with the program, she wasn't a Muppets fan and hadn't really watched them. She knew it was a long shot at best, but she pressed on.

Once at the audition, she and the others got improv assignments, and she did okay, though her Muppet work was lame, with her puppet basically flopping around. Once the auditions were completed, Henson chose twenty artists. Fifteen were selected for advanced training plus some immediate work on the show, and five, including Camille, were assigned to a six-week, introductory workshop led by Henson (who played Kermit, Rowlf, etc.), Kevin Clash (Elmo, Clifford, etc.), and Richard Hunt (Scooter, Beaker, etc.), who later died of AIDS.

A one-on-one interview with Henson was part of the audition, and Camille impressed him with her lack of pretension. She admitted her exposure to the Muppets phenomenon came mainly through the Miss Piggy mugs and calendars her friends had. He smiled when she said this and ended up hiring her on the spot.

Fortunately, they were looking for more women to join the troupe. They had one from the UK and a couple from America (compared to a total of fifteen men), and they were pleased another woman with Camille's gifts was available. So, they trained and incorporated her, and she saw God's providence at work, for it offered her a chance to do clean comedy and stay in New York.

She was gifted in accents, and she cultivated them as Henson threw ideas her way. One time, the *Sesame Street* writers started with a name gag, "Meryl Sheep," and she did her homework on the actress, study that included renting *Sophie's Choice*, which inspired her to take up Streep's Polish accent. She nailed it, and the character (one of several she developed through her dozen years with the show) took hold.[15] In January of 1998, *People* magazine did a feature on the character, and in November of that year, she appeared with the Count on the *Today Show*.

People reported:

> Meryl Sheep is at it again. Big Bird is staging a production of Little Bo Peep, and he wants her to play one of the sheep. As is her wont, however, Meryl rejects the typecasting and will settle for nothing less than the lead. "But how can a sheep be Bo Peep?" asks Big Bird. Clearing her throat and replying in an Eastern European accent … Sheep answers, "I am an actress, dahling. I can be anything I choose."

> What she's chosen to be—indisputably—is the most talked-about new character (and most mutton-headed actress) on TV. Created in part by Sesame Street's head writer, Norman Stiles, Sheep has had nothing but ewelogies since her debut. The latest in a long line of Sesame's celeb-based creatures, such as Alistair Cookie and Placido Flamingo, Meryl weaves together the to-dye-for looks of Shari Lewis' Lamb Chop and the if-looks-could-kill temperament of Joan Collins. The combination has given the adults among Sesame Street's 12 million-weekly audience an even better excuse to watch the show. "It's a privilege to work with such a talent," says Stiles, 45, who writes some of Meryl's material. "I don't think there's a greater talent anywhere on four hooves" … "She's a bit demanding at times," admits puppeteer Camille Bonora, who's also had a big hand in Meryl's career.[16]

Though a key member of the team, Camille was something of an "eccentric" due to her Christian commitments. In London for an Easter special, she wouldn't join the script readings on Sunday until after church; she didn't follow the others in dabbling in New Age stuff, Est, Tai Chi, or Scientology; and she was celibate, refusing to date people who weren't saved (earning the nickname, "No-Deal Camille"), with Jim Henson as no exception. He was estranged from his wife and "a bit of a ladies' man." When he asked Camille if they could meet for dinner to discuss business, she declined, but offered to take him to lunch.

She also stuck her neck out to urge changes in the script when she thought the words might not be so good for the kids. For instance, in a day when Santeria was getting big play in the press, they came down with a song warning, "Don't do this, or you'll turn into a witch's shoe." She didn't think it was good to make light of the occult, so she suggested they go with "…you'll turn into a bugaboo," with a Little Bugaboo puppet—and 'bugaboo' turned out to be more fun. They'd already fashioned the set and costumes for the witch theme, but they made the change.

In a similar vein, Camille had on occasion played the Countess to Count von Count (modeled on Bela Lugosi's version of the vampire, Dracula), but she asked to be excused from that role. She'd heard that Anton LaVey, founder of the Church of Satan, had been fascinated with vampires when he was a child, and she didn't want to encourage associations with that dark-side narrative.

Camille's consecration was not simply a matter of distancing herself from sub-Christian themes. She also integrated her faith with the details of her work, as when the director did the countdown to begin taping. She'd whisper lines from Psalm 121 in the gaps:

"Counting down, five …"
"I will lift up my eyes unto the hills …"
"Four …"

"Where does my help come from?"
"Three …"
"My help comes from the Lord …"
"Two …"
"The Maker of heaven and earth."
"One."[17]

The crew saw her lips moving and supposed she was nervously rehearsing her lines.

In 1990, when Jim Henson died suddenly of streptococcal pneumonia at fifty-three, many of the cast members took part in the funeral. (Henson had abandoned the Christian Science faith of his youth, but it's reasonable to think vestiges of that upbringing kept him from seeking immediate medical aid, which could have saved him.) As the Muppeteers and their characters walked down the aisle and, at the end of the service, assembled on the platform to sing, "If Just One Person Believes in You," Camille sang through her now-classic character, Meryl Sheep.[18] (While in good health a year or so earlier, Henson had requested this song for his funeral, not knowing how short his remaining time was to be.)

CHAPTER 8

"Could Somebody Help Me?" (The "Leahs")

As a young Christian, Camille happened upon a ministry she continues to this day, care for the elderly. It started one Sunday morning when she was waiting at a bus stop. A blind lady approached, swinging her stick from side to side, and when the bus arrived, she asked, "Could somebody help me?" Camille jumped in to assist her, and they talked a bit. As they were about to part, she offered to call to see if there was anything else she might do. Instead, Leah asked for Camille's number, which she took down in Braille, entering it with a stylus, using a special template.

She was an elderly, poor, half-deaf, Jewish, Charismatic Christian, and Camille "became a daughter" to her. Camille helped her with grocery shopping and keeping her financial affairs in order—no small challenge. Though a resident of Section 8 Housing (with government rental assistance for low-income households), Leah was continually giving away money, especially in response to mailed appeals. She was living on only $600 a month but would send $5 here and $5 there. When Camille pressed her to be more cautious, she replied, "Okay, but remember, you can't outgive God."

Camille also took care of her at her death, a passing for which Leah was prepared. As she put it, "The first thing I'll see is Jesus." (Leah often reminded people cheerfully, "Keep looking up because Jesus is looking down"; that's how she witnessed.)

On the day when Camille and Mano were wed (again, a jump ahead in the narrative), Camille wasn't available to help Leah cut her meat at the reception. So, she asked fellow Muppeteer, Joey Mazzarino, an observant Catholic, to sit with Leah and help her. (He was the right hand of the puppet character Eddie in the *Ben and Eddie* series Camille produced in the 1990s.) He, too, struck up a friendship with Leah and became something of a son to her. When he told her, "You may be blind, but you taught us to see," she responded, "I'm not blind, I'm sightless. The blind don't know Jesus."

"Invisible" Marguerite and Joan

Through her work with Leah, Camille came to agree with Regent College professor James Houston when he said that, while the challenge of the early church was to help the poor across the board, the challenge of the church today is to help care for the elderly. She believes they are—in a sense—invisible to the Western world, and churches need to "adopt" them the way Christians adopt kids in India. For one thing, she suggests volunteers should be paired with seniors and visit them regularly.

With this conviction, Camille has gone on to help other seniors in dire circumstances, a ministry that continues to this day. Another case in point is Marguerite, who endured the Nazi occupation of Europe, had been abused by two husbands, and had suffered a nervous breakdown. Camille reached out to her when she saw her rocking in her seat anxiously in church. Over the next several years, she took her to concerts and other public events, and, within five years or so, Marguerite was socializing with a good measure of comfort.

As Marguerite's health declined, Camille gave a woman named Joan some money to sit with her two or three hours at a time. This worked well for the first two years, but in the third year, Joan began slipping into dementia, and Camille began to help her too. For one thing, she couldn't write a check properly, and collection agencies were after her; she'd write "Rent" after "Pay to," and it wouldn't go through. And she didn't know what a credit line was; she thought it was a statement of her account balance and was delighted to see the number growing as it rose to cover her debts. Camille asked for Joan's check book and wrote checks for her for three months. When she went to the bank, they expressed their gratitude and asked if they could call her with questions and concerns as they arose, and she agreed.

When she saw Joan walking on the sides of her feet, she learned her toenails were bothering her. Told she needed a pedicure, Joan, in her confusion, assured Camille that she visited the salon regularly. When Camille took her to one, the ladies were horrified. Her toenails were animal-like, curled and discolored, extending an inch or so beyond the toes. There was also infection. The workers immediately declined the job, but referred her to a podiatrist, who found extensive infection in the bone of one of the toes and treated it for months.

This isn't to say Joan was "homebound," for she had a gratifying routine, which took her to a particular restaurant (where everybody knew her, as well as her standard fare—Pepsi, matzo ball soup, and a roll), to church, and to the hairdresser (which she began visiting weekly instead of six-weekly). Since the diner was Greek, Camille had rapport with the manager since she'd become somewhat familiar with the language. (But again, we get ahead of ourselves.)

As dementia took its toll, Joan lost track of the demands of personal hygiene. When Camille first came to her apartment, she noticed the shower handle didn't work and there were no signs of usage. The sheets were so dirty they had to be thrown away, and she had to put on gloves to pre-soak-and-rinse the laundry until the water ran clear before putting it into the machine. Later, an attendant named Miriam came by three times a week to make sure Joan and her things stayed clean. (Of course, this sort of ministry was early fruit of Camille's salvation, for, though she was still in the "me-centered" entertainment world, she'd found life in serving others.)

Denville Hall

Along the way, Camille found fellowship with others sharing her concern for the elderly. Once, in Bermuda, she and Mano were attending a dinner party arranged to introduce a guest from England and his girlfriend. Over dinner, the guest mentioned that his partner ran a retirement home, and Camille's interest was piqued. Providentially, the hostess had people change places for dessert, Camille found herself seated beside this lady, and the two had a great conversation on this issue.

The lady, named Lala, had appeared in two seasons of *Doctor Who* and had also been Richard Dawkins' third wife. Her "home for the elderly" was Denville Hall, a retirement destination for actors, actresses, and others in the theatrical profession. It counts Sir Richard Attenborough, Pat Coombs (of the 1971 *Willy Wonka & the Chocolate Factory*), Brenda Cowling (who played a teacher in the 1982 *Pink Floyd—The Wall*) as residents, and its list of financial supporters has included Sean Connery, Michael Caine, and Elizabeth Taylor.

Lala lamented the fact that, for the most part, British actors were not so generous in this cause, in contrast with American support for such enterprises as the Motion Picture & Television Country House and Hospital in Los Angeles, for which Kirk Douglas made a $15 million gift.

Camille was struck by her thoughtfulness and creativity. For instance, one of the problems was that people with dementia would get up and wander about the property in the middle of the night. When they awoke and saw the staff in day clothes, they figured it was time to get up. So, the employees began wearing pajamas, allowing them to say with plausibility, "What are you doing up? It's bedtime," and the residents would return more readily to their rooms.

Camille as Eliza Doolittle in *My Fair Lady* at Gonzaga High School in DC
(Photo by Gonzaga College High School.)

Christine Anderson
Camille Bonora
Bob Calvo
Joe Clonick
Billy Padgett
Suzanne Smartt
Karl Tiedemann

LAFFING MATTERS

FORMERLY *Play by Play*

THEY'RE BACK AND BETTER THAN EVER!

THREE MONDAYS in APRIL — 13th, 20th, 27th

$3.00   9:00 p.m.

Refreshments Available

CHICAGO CITY LIMITS IMPROVISATIONAL THEATRE
By Theatre Row. 534 W. 42 St. 695-2351

Comedy Tonight!

Camille with Jim Henson on the *Sesame Street* set

Camille with First Lady, Barbara Bush, and "Gordon Robinson" (Roscoe Orman)

Camille on the set of *Ben and Eddie*

MANO AND CAMILLE TOGETHER

CHAPTER 9

"I Can't See You This Week."
(Mano and Camille Become a Team.)

As Camille transitioned to Times Square Church, Ben Harney introduced her to Karalyn Schuchert, wife of Joseph Schuchert, the Kelso Group executive who worked with Mano at American Standard and who had invited him to the church. Karalyn took her under her wing, and the two of them had lunch together regularly. But one day, Karalyn called to say, "I can't see you this week. We're ministering to Emmanuel Kampouris, who lost his wife. Joe's bringing him to church, and we're taking him a covered dish meal."

Brunches and the Philharmonic

Before long, Camille met this Kampouris fellow at one of the brunches the Schucherts held at their home after church. She found him "gentlemanly," but there was no sense in either of them that they might become man and wife in the not-too-distant future. For one thing, he would be overseas for a time, traveling to Mount Athos in August.

The next significant contact came at the end of a Times Square service, when Karalyn asked Camille to keep Mano company for a time, there in the auditorium, before they all headed to brunch. She needed about twenty minutes to help some attendees she'd met, and she wanted to be sure Mano wasn't left in the lurch. Indeed, Karalyn saw herself as something of a mother to Mano in this period of his life, concerned for his care. That was all she had in mind with this request. She didn't see this as an opening move in matchmaking. Karalyn knew Camille didn't date, and she considered her a "safe" option when it was natural that others might have designs on this widower.

Though Karalyn did not intend to pair Mano and Camille with a look to the future, she also provided the next big opportunity for their relationship to develop. The occasion was the debut of New York Philharmonic conductor Kurt Masur, set for September 11, 1991, at Lincoln Center. (Masur served until 2002, having succeeded Zubin Mehta, who had led the Philharmonic for thirteen years.) The Schucherts had bought tickets for the performance and reserved a table for the pre-concert dinner, and Karalyn wanted to be sure Mano, their guest, had someone to accompany him.

She first asked the aforementioned actress Diane Venora, but she couldn't go. So, she asked Mano if he had a suggestion, and he asked, "What about that Bonora girl, the one I talked to after the service?" And so she called Camille, telling her she'd already tried Diane, assuring her it was "absolutely not a date," and saying she'd seat her next to Joe rather than Mano at the concert. But the dinner organizers had a different plan, and she found herself beside Mano at the table, with plenty of opportunity for conversation. It proved to be an important event in the budding of their relationship. (Camille remembers the evening in detail, including his getting her some sparkling water before the lights went down for the performance.)

She was struck by Mano's fascination with prayer. He asked how she prayed and what she prayed for, and he told her about his own experience at the monastery, how he'd met "men who were so unattached to this world." In her heart, she said, "Wow!"

In November, he asked her to Sunday brunch, and they ended up spending the afternoon together, from 1:00 to 5:00 p.m., returning to the night service at Times Square. And the meetings were not limited to Sundays. One weekday, Camille told him she was suffering from bronchitis, and he took her for soup at the Carlyle (the luxury, Upper East Side, residential hotel, where President Kennedy had an apartment, hence the nickname, "New York White House").

She was thirty-five and he fifty-six, but they found themselves of "one heart and one mind." Her longtime friend, Brenda Bass, after hearing Camille talk to Mano on the phone, observed, "This is the one. I've never seen you so totally yourself." And, indeed, Camille had come to genuinely love—and like—Mano.

As things got serious, he said he had to tell her three things: (1) that he had suffered deep grief; (2) that when he recently awakened during the night and gotten on his knees for prayer, the grief lifted, and her face came to mind; and (3) that he wanted her to be his wife.

The Counsel of Wilkerson and Phillips

With this striking development, she ran to Pastor Wilkerson for counsel. (She'd been saying, as a confirmed single, she was "married to Jesus," not suspecting that she would one day be married to "Emmanuel.") He said, "Camille, he's like a Cornelius [the centurion in Acts]. He'll need someone to walk beside him. Don't put him under a microscope. Take three months to decide." And then he prayed, "If there's any guile in him, please let me know." Wilkerson had had lunch with him, and there he observed that "he doesn't know the Word, but he'll learn that. The question is, 'Does he love God?'"

She also turned to Bob Phillips, and he said there were four things she needed to consider: (1) his age; (2) his life (for she would marry his life and his social circle); (3) the children (for such relationships are not always easy); and (4) whether he had grieved enough (and Bob thought he had). As for (3), Camille recounts that, though there have been challenges, as with any blending of families and personalities, their "lives have been enriched and blessed" by Mano's two sons

(Andrew and Alexander), their wives (Sarah and Ivey), and five wonderful grandchildren (Myrto, Timothy, and Madeleine by Andrew and Sarah; Emmanuel and Elena by Alexander and Ivey). And so, the praying and reflecting and counseling proceeded.

In due course, on March 7, 1992, Mano and Camille were married at St. George Greek Orthodox Church on Manhattan's West 54th Street, with the Orthodox priest presiding, with Bob Phillips preaching, and David Wilkerson in attendance.

CHAPTER 10
"Have You Met Eric?" (Socrates/Christ in the City)

Among the young media professionals Camille met at Times Square Church was Eric Metaxas, who'd begun attending in the early 1990s. At the time, he was working for Rabbit Ears Entertainment (and, of course, he has subsequently written a wide range of material for publishers as diverse as *Veggie Tales*, the *New York Times*, and Thomas Nelson, who published his best-selling biography of Dietrich Bonhoeffer).

In those days, a group of singles "on fire for the Lord" would go out for pizza and talk about their faith and its application to their life and work. So, it was natural for them to get acquainted.

Eric remembers that when Mano came into her life and they were married, he expected this "captain of industry," who was closer to his own parents' age, to be august or distant, but he "was surprised at how much fun he was." Mano's and Camille's wedding—"Times Square Meets Orthodox"—fit Eric's Orthodox/Evangelical "DNA" perfectly, he of Greek descent and evangelical present. (We, on the *KJ* crew can testify to the "fun Mano was." For instance, I found an old email from 2003, where he passed along some nutty headlines, including "Red Tape Holds Up New Bridge" and "Kids Make Nutritious Snacks.")

Socrates in the City

A number of years later, Eric was working with Stan Oakes, the president of King's College, to raise funds for Socrates in the City (designed "to create a forum that might encourage busy professionals in thinking about the bigger questions in life"), and they approached the Kampourises for support. Hoping to enlist them as one of many donors, they were astonished to hear they'd finance the whole enterprise, with Eric as director, for a year and a half. And so, they put Socrates on the map.

A big theme of this book is the fruit bearing on many branches, thanks to God's work with and through the Kampourises. One such linkup occurred when the Kampourises took the *Kairos Journal* team (a group to be introduced later) to a Socrates event at New York's St. Regis Hotel. David Aikman, the former senior foreign correspondent for *Time* magazine was the speaker, with Eric presiding. After his talk and the Q&A that followed, a number of us gathered for dinner in a room downstairs, and the conversation continued. It was there Eric met Greg Thornbury, and a friendship developed. Little did they know that a decade later, Greg would come as president of King's College and they would be members of what Eric calls the "Clapham Sect" for the less-than-evangelical City of New York.

Occasionally, our Kairos team would find itself in New York for work at the same time as a Socrates in the City gathering, and we'd head over to the program. On one of these dates, March 25, 2004, Socrates met at the University Club to hear Paul Vitz, a professor of psychology at NYU. I'd heard him back in the 1980s at a Catholic apologetics conference, meeting under a big circus tent at Franciscan University in Steubenville, Ohio. There, he spoke of the absence or failings of the fathers of prominent atheists. He later wrote a book on the psychology of atheism.[19] This particular evening in New York, he picked up on the same general topic with "The Importance of Fatherhood."

Though the issue was very serious, Eric started things light, as was his wont:

> My introductions have always been dopey—or dippy—because we firmly believe that's the surest way of letting the audience and the speaker know up front that we expect to have fun and that this will not be a ponderous intellectual exercise. We will not abide pretentiousness, but we will sometimes countenance a freewheeling Marx Brothers approach to the search for truth. To this point, my opening comments and introductions have often taken their cues from the speeches of Foster Brooks and Charlie Callas at Dean Martin's celebrity roasts. This was intentional. After all, who said that the exploration of the Big Questions and fun can't go together? It was probably La Rochefoucauld, but who cares what he thinks? Seriously, I think that the fun we have is vital to what we do. We know that no matter how serious the subject (suffering and evil and death, for example), we will enjoy ourselves ... My philosophy is that answering the Big Questions about "life, God, and other small topics" can be fun if you know in advance that there are actually good and hopeful answers to those questions.[20]

As for Vitz, Eric remarked that he was their first New York speaker as he ran through the list of others, noting DC resident Os Guinness had spoken eight times—"a Guinness world record."[21]

In 2003, he'd introduced Sir John Polkinghorne as "KBE [Knight of the British Empire], FRS [Companions of Honor, established by George V], DDS [Doctor of Dental Science, which Polkinghorne was not, for his doctorate was in physics, a topic he'd taught at Cambridge], and Notorious B.I.G."—with Metaxas observing,

"That's a typo. That's a hip-hop joke. I don't expect you to get it, Dr. Polkinghorne."

That same year, he'd introduced Boston College philosophy professor Peter Kreeft (another speaker I'd heard in Steubenville) by saying,

> Perhaps one big question many of us have here to-night is whether the speaker's name is pronounced "Kr*ee*ft" or Kr*ay*ft." At least it was for me. In dealing with Dr. "Krayft" over the phone, I have come to hear him say "Krayft" a number of times, and I just sort of assumed he would know. So whether he is right or wrong, we will just follow his lead and drop that question going forward.

And then there was Father Richard John Neuhaus, asked to speak "on the fabulously provocative subject of whether an atheist can be a good citizen. I think the short answer might be 'yes,' but I look forward to Father Neuhaus's more in-depth and nuanced thinking on this subject." Before Neuhaus spoke, Eric observed (quite bogusly), "I would, of course, be remiss in failing to mention that tonight's festivities, which are heavily subsidized, are brought to you by Bounty, the quicker picker-upper. Also by Amana, makers of the Amana Radar Range: If it doesn't say, 'Amana,' it's not a Radar Range."

And there were others who got the Metaxas-intro treatment: He took pains to distinguish Chuck Colson from Chaka Khan: "Chaka Khan is a singer of funk. Chuck Colson is *not* a singer of funk." Francis Collins was head of the Human Genome Project, not the Human Gnome Project. As for Collins's honors,

> In 2003, his was the *Biography of the Year* on the A&E network, for which he beat out Valerie Bertinelli by one vote ... Incredible. I think she was in the middle of divorcing Eddie Van Halen. It was a big year for her, but he still beat her out. This was the man who

could do that in that year. The year when everybody was talking, "Bertinelli, Bertinelli," he beat her out by one vote. I'm in awe of that …

Paul Vitz

But silliness aside, back to Vitz, who asked,

> What is the father's major function? … [T]he father is a kind of Mr. Outside, while the mother is Mr. Inside. She forms the basic character, the emotional life, the interpersonal responsiveness of the child, much more than the father. But the father introduces the child much more often to the outside world. The father symbolizes the structure of that world, of law and order, of the activities, of the things that you get involved in when you leave the home.

Speaking of criminality:

> This is perhaps the major way in which failed fathers pass on their sins to the next generation. There are plenty of poor environments where the fathers are present and there is no criminality. We think of criminal behavior as somehow related to ghettos or the inner city or something like that. When the social scientists take out whether the father is present and the whole issue of the stability of the family, there are no ethnic, racial, linguistic, or cultural factors related to criminal behavior. It is family structure that counts, and the crucial family person that isn't there is the father. The mother may be there, but she commonly struggles through welfare; if she has a job, the children get farmed out to daycare. Either way, there's a big price to pay for the children.

Vitz then picked up on the spiritual aspect, drawing examples from his earlier work on the psychology of atheism: the god-denying Ludwig Feuerbach (who impacted Karl Marx), whose father (a man of volcanic temper) abandoned the family in Ludwig's early teens, fathered a child through his best friend's wife, and then returned to the family when that woman died; Arthur Schopenhauer, whose father, often absent, committed suicide; Thomas Hobbes, whose third-rate Anglican clergyman father beat up another clergyman in front of the church and then ran off, never to be seen again; Sigmund Freud, who saw his father as a milquetoast and a sexual pervert; Voltaire, whose made-up name broke ties with the family name, and whose first play was titled *Oedipe* (Oedipus); Friedrich Nietzsche, whose father died when he was four; Madalyn Murray O'Hair, who once threatened her father with a butcher's knife, saying, "I want to kill you; I want to dance on your grave"; and others such as Jean-Paul Sartre, David Hume, and Bertrand Russell "who fit the pattern of the dead father and the absence of any good substitute father."[22]

Gadfly

Needless to say, such arguments for the traditional family didn't rise naturally from the New York culture, but were "gadfly" notions, posed in the tradition of Socrates, who so irritated the elites in Athens he was condemned to death for "corrupting the youth" with his provocative questioning.

As for Metaxas, he continues to address the culture, both contemporary and historic, both highs and lows, whether through his books (biographical works on Luther, Wilberforce, and Bonhoeffer), his radio program (the *Eric Metaxas Show*), or his efforts to bring the Bonhoeffer story to film.

CHAPTER 11

Gordon MacDonald Cites Wilberforce.
(The Road to *Kairos Journal*)

Early in their marriage, Mano began attending a Tuesday luncheon for businessmen, meeting at St. Bartholomew's Episcopal Church ("St. Bart's") on Park Avenue. It was led by a rotation of ministers—Tim Keller, Gordon McDonald, and a messianic rabbi from New Jersey. Their messages were strictly limited to thirty minutes, and the effect was compelling. Before long, the Kampourises were attending Trinity Baptist Church, on the same block on West 57th Street as Carnegie Hall, and it was here they learned of a nineteenth-century member of the English Parliament named William Wilberforce.

Today, Wilberforce, who led the successful charge against slavery in the British Empire, is something of a household name among Evangelicals, thanks in part to Eric Metaxas's 2007 biography, *Amazing Grace*, and the film of that name released in America that same year. But, in 1993, Wilberforce was not on the Kampouris's radar, and they were intrigued, determined to dig deeper. In 1998, with the help of McDonald's successor at Trinity, Keith Boyd, they learned a good deal about this Christian statesman, including the fact that his pastor, John Venn, was a major influence in his life.

Murphy Brown

They began to think more and more about the way the church could shape society, and, in this vein, they threw support behind Vice President Dan Quayle's run for the presidency in 2000. They especially appreciated his advocacy for traditional family values (for which, in 1992, he was vilified in the media for speaking ill of television character Murphy Brown's breezy approach to out-of-wedlock motherhood).

A measure of vindication came in April 1993, when *The Atlantic* published an article by Barbara Defoe Whitehead, entitled shockingly and gratifyingly, "Dan Quayle Was Right."[23] The editor's introduction reads:

> The social-science evidence is in: though it may benefit the adults involved, the dissolution of intact two-parent families is harmful to large numbers of children. Moreover, the author argues, family diversity in the form of increasing numbers of single-parent and stepparent families does not strengthen the social fabric but, rather, dramatically weakens and undermines society.

Whitehead then substantiates the title with a range of statistics and implications, such as these which honor the perspective of both Quayle and the Kampourises:

- Children in single-parent families are six times as likely to be poor.

- Contrary to popular belief, many children do not "bounce back" after divorce.

- If we fail to come to terms with the relationship between family structure and declining child well-being, then it will be increasingly difficult to improve children's life prospects, no matter how many new programs the federal government funds.

- [B]oth cohabiting and remarried couples are more likely to break up than couples in first marriages.

- In recent years, some people have argued these trends pose a serious threat to children and the nation as a whole, but they are dismissed as declinists, pessimists, or nostalgists, unwilling or unable to accept the new facts of life. The dominant view is that the changes in family structure are, on balance, positive.

- What had once been regarded as hostile to children's best interests was now considered essential to adults' happiness.

- Madison Avenue and Hollywood did not invent these behaviors, as their highly-paid publicists are quick to point out, but they have played an influential role in defending and even celebrating divorce and unwed motherhood. More precisely, they have taken the raw material of demography and fashioned it into a powerful fantasy of individual renewal and rebirth.

- Even the conservative bastion of the greeting-card industry, Hallmark, offers a line of cards commemorating divorce as liberation.

- As this story shows, unwed parenthood is thought of not only as a way to find happiness but also as a way to exhibit such virtues as honesty and courage … Murphy was not just exercising her rights as a woman; she was exhibiting true moral heroism.

- Increasingly, the media depicts the married two-parent family as a source of pathology. According to a spate of celebrity memoirs and interviews, the married parent family harbors terrible secrets of abuse, violence, and incest.

- In 1976, less than half as many fathers as in 1957 said providing for children was a life goal. The proportion of working men who found marriage and children burdensome and restrictive more than doubled in the same period. Fewer than half of all adult Americans today regard the idea of sacrifice for others as a positive moral virtue.

- Over the past two and a half decades Americans have been conducting what is tantamount to a vast natural experiment in family life ... The results of the experiment are coming in, and they are clear ... [T]his is the first generation in the nation's history to do worse psychologically, socially, and economically than its parents.

The Quayle Campaign

When Quayle ran for president in 1999, Mano chaired his eighty-member finance committee.[24] The critical difference was George W. Bush's entry into the race, he the son of the president whom Quayle had served as vice-president. At that point, support coalesced around the Texas governor. Still, the Quayle campaign sounded important themes, with a handout declaring that his "agenda for America's future is grounded in the same conservative, pro-family, pro-growth principles he has stood for throughout his life and public service."

It went on to say that, among other things, he'd work for lower taxes ("No country can remain great if it burdens its people with high taxes, complex rules, and an out-of-control bureaucracy."); a more secure America (undoing "the damage" of "the Clinton-Gore Administration"); community renewal (believing "big government is *not* the solution" to drug abuse, teen pregnancy, crime, and the breakup of the family); a better educated America (through such measures as "education savings accounts," "charter schools," and "periodic testing of teachers"); regulatory and legal reform (including insistence on sound science for regulations and a "loser pays" rule to discourage frivolous lawsuits). He concluded by saying that "the test of a great country is its willingness to advance basic values that have withstood the test of time that protect the most vulnerable among us; that embody the best we have to offer."

In the course of Quayle's campaign, the Kampourises were dismayed at the indifference of the churches, including those of their evangelical tribe, to address public policy matters. He asked Pastor Bob, "Why aren't people saying more?" and they began to discuss these matters. From this frustration grew fresh resolve to make a difference, working with pastors rather than politicians, in the hope their ministries would turn their congregants' eyes to the great moral causes of this world. And so was born the notion of *Kairos Journal*, designed to encourage, equip, and embolden pastors to engage the culture prophetically.

John Venn's example through the Clapham Sect was strong motivation for this new publishing venture, and his story on the journal's pages would soon be joined by others, such as Andre Trocme´ (a French Protestant pastor who shielded Jews from the Nazis); Jean-Baptiste Massillon (a French Catholic bishop who preached rebuke to Louis XIV and Louis XV); and New York pastor Charles Henry Parkhurst, who took on the corrupt Tammany Hall in the late nineteenth century.

The Kairos Moment

Once the journal was established, we began to spread the word through a brochure, a video, and print ads. (Some of us got into the act with ad copy, my own contribution being the expression, "A Prophetable Meeting" sitting above a cluster of names represented on the site—Cyprian, Tozer, Moody, Calvin, Wesley, Basil, Kierkegaard, Schaeffer, Luther, Ryle, Edwards, Blamires, Kuyper, Bede, Trueblood, Dabney, etc.)

The video, *The Kairos Moment*, began by displaying a collage of words—"Prophetic … God-Given … Unique … Current … Propitious … Time … Season … Decisive …" and then offered a definition:

> KAIROS: N. [GRK] … A SINGULAR MOMENT, DEMANDING A DETERMINED RESPONSE FROM GOD'S PEOPLE; A CROSSROADS IN TIME; A UNIQUE OPPORTUNITY, EITHER SEIZED—OR LOST FOREVER.

This was followed by the text of 2 Timothy 4:2:

> PREACH THE WORD: BE PREPARED IN SEASON AND OUT OF SEASON; CONVICE, REBUKE, EXHORT WITH ALL LONGSUFFERING AND TEACHING.

Over ancient Christian paintings, the narrator began, "For centuries, Christian men and women have brought eternity into time by speaking the Word of God to the surrounding culture. And where the Church has been faithful to the task, the result has been a world turned upside down." Later, he underscored the importance of the pulpit: "The spirit of the age seems to find good works more palatable than good preaching, but the two are inextricably connected."

The video was peppered with strong images and quotes—Cyprian and Jerome on gladiatorial games; Clement of Alexandria on infanticide; Chrysostom on care for the poor; Lord Henry Peter Brougham of the Clapham Sect on slavery; Lord Shaftesbury on child labor; Martin Luther King on racial segregation; Dorothy Sayers on the importance of theology to morality; and four Anglican archbishops from the Global South on sexual immorality and the moral decline of the Global North Church.

Nearing the finale, the text of Ezekiel 22:30 appeared on screen:

SO I SOUGHT FOR A MAN AMONG THEM
WHO WOULD MAKE A WALL, AND STAND
IN THE GAP BEFORE ME ON BEHALF OF THE
LAND, THAT I SHOULD NOT DESTROY IT.

The video concluded with the Kairos logo bearing the words, "FOR SUCH A TIME AS THIS …"

CHAPTER 12

"You Need to Visit St. Michael's, Chester Square."
(Building a Team of Brits)

When at their home in northern New Jersey, the Kampourises attended a Christian Missionary Alliance church, where they met Grace Wort, who soon moved to London to work through Campus Crusade for Christ. The ministry, called *Agape*, was directed toward the city's "Wall Street types," whom she invited to low-key evangelistic dinners. Mano sponsored some of these gatherings, and the Kampourises attended one. While in London on that occasion, Grace brought them to her church, St. Michael's, Chester Square, where they first met Charles Marnham and his wife Tricia. It proved to be a signal encounter, as Grace suspected it would be.

St. Michael's is situated in the exclusive Belgravia district of London. The Marnhams' row-house vicarage, just down the street, stands next to the former residence of the nineteenth-century poet Matthew Arnold and bears a commemorative blue plaque. Former Prime Minister Margaret Thatcher lived just across the Square's garden.

During those years, St. Michael's had many Americans in the congregation; indeed, at one time, they had almost more Americans than Brits. They were usually bankers or corporate lawyers who had come over for three to five years with their young families. They'd been devastated by the attacks of 9/11 and, being so far from home, had come to see Charles and Tricia as almost *in loco parentis*. And the Marnhams formed a strong affection for them and most things American.

The Alpha Course

Charles and Tricia had served earlier at Holy Trinity, Brompton, in London's Knightsbridge neighborhood, and it was there they were recognized for an extraordinary accomplishment, the creation of the Alpha Course, an evangelistic and discipleship program with trans-denominational usage around the world. It began over a meal at Charles and Tricia's first meeting in 1977.

Tricia, a native of Northern Ireland, had a Covenanter background, and had majored in French and Spanish at Scotland's St. Andrews University. From there, she'd gone on to work for the Bank of England in London, for British InterVarsity Fellowship (now called UCCF, the Universities and Colleges Christian Fellowship), and for the Billy Graham Evangelistic Association in Brussels. Then she'd undertaken legal studies for the office of solicitor and found her way to Holy Trinity, where she was serving on the church council. She became concerned over the growing number of new Christians who needed training in the basics of the faith. When she mentioned this to the vicar (senior minister) Raymond Turvey, he said that a new-curate (trainee vicar) Charles Marnham was about to arrive, and he could address it.

Charles was, indeed, the man, and after a delay of some weeks due to scheduling conflicts, he and Tricia finally met for breakfast. The meeting went so well that it extended into lunch. Together, they hatched the notion of basic training for new believers, with Tricia suggesting the name "Alpha" to fit the notion of beginnings.

The six-week course began in the autumn of 1977 with eight people. There would be a short talk on a topic such as "Who was Jesus?" with a paper handout including all the relevant Bible references. The talk would be followed by discussion, with only one rule: There is no question you cannot ask.

Although the course was aimed at new believers, God had bigger plans for it. Tricia and another colleague attempted at the same time to initiate an evangelistic course for enquirers, but it attracted only four people and was soon shut down. It was clear that God intended Alpha to be both an evangelistic and a basic discipleship course, which it is to this day.

Over the next thirteen years, the course was extended, with various Holy Trinity staff members adding material. Then, Nicky Gumbel arrived and further refined the course, which went global in the 1990s. But the original format remains the same: refreshments (now generally a meal); teaching; a handout (now a professionally-designed and -produced manual); and the all-important group discussion.

The ask-any-question rule was particularly important to Charles, who, as a Cambridge student (in law and art history), was frustrated when the church didn't address his questions or provided answers to questions he hadn't asked. He was yet to be converted, and his big question was, "What is a Christian?" Instead, he was hearing only "wonderful abstractions."

By God's grace, someone sent him to Mark Ruston, the vicar of The Church of the Holy Sepulchre (popularly known as The Round Church) in Cambridge, where Ruston took him through a six-week course focusing on the Cross. On January 29, 1971 (a date Charles recites without pause), he moved from being a "believer" to a "Christian," as he puts it. And later, Ruston, who had steered many men toward the priesthood, encouraged Charles to take that path.

So the one-time questioner made sure that Alpha gave generous space for the questions dogging attendees. And Charles has fielded a lot of interesting ones through the years, some of them off the wall. University students take the lead in this connection, prompting him to ask himself and sometimes them, "Where did that come from?" One of his favorite and most effective answers is to steer them to "the resource documents" (namely the Bible). They've been steeped in that standard, pertinent to their study of history or the classics, and it's fair to press them this direction when they're (mis)construing Christianity this way or that.

What Can I Do To Help?

Little did the Kampourises and Marnhams know at their first meeting in London that they would become teammates in the work of *Kairos Journal*. The Kampourises were yet to hear Gordon McDonald speak of William Wilberforce or be inspired by the example of Wilberforce's pastor John Venn. They'd not yet worked on the Dan Quayle presidential campaign and experienced the apathy of Christian voters.

In 2002, Mano came to Charles with his bold notion for an online journal, one that could help pastors preach more meaningfully to their congregations on the national and cultural issues of the day. Charles picked up on the idea right away. As he recalls, the conversation went like this:

> Mano: I am passionate about the importance of the local church.
> Charles: That's great!
> Mano: I want to set up a website to assist pastors in their ministry, in particular with respect to speaking into the public square.
> Charles: Wonderful!
> Mano: The website would be free for pastors.
> Charles: What can I do to help?

Before long, Charles and Tricia agreed to host a Kairos presentation at St. Michael's, and several evangelical leaders accepted the invitation—John Stott's successor at All Souls, Langham Place, Richard Bews; Martyn Lloyd-Jones's daughter Elizabeth, and her husband, Sir Fred Catherwood; Michael Schluter of The Relationships Foundation; and Greg Haslam, senior pastor of Westminster Chapel, where Martyn Lloyd-Jones had ministered some years before. So the Kampourises, Doug Baker (whom you'll meet in the next chapter), and Bob Phillips headed to London, armed with fresh website graphics (thanks to Gil Lavelanet) and a custom-built data base (thanks to Mano's nephew, the Canadian Dimitri Kampouris).

The chief result of that meeting was the deepening of Charles's commitment to the project. (He was encouraged in this by another meeting attendee, a young pastor from a very isolated situation in Wales who commented enthusiastically, "This is exactly what we need!") Charles went on to introduce them to some key contacts, including David Jackman, Director of the Proclamation Trust; journalist/economist Rachel Tingle; and, via Derek Tidball (the then-Principal of the London School of Theology), Peter Riddell, an expert on Islam, who was to add strategic writings to the *Kairos Journal* corpus. (Riddell, then a professor at the London School of Theology, is now the vice-principal of the Melbourne School of Theology.)

Vaughan Roberts

After the meeting, the American team drove down to Oxford for tea with Vaughan Roberts, vicar of St. Ebbe's, and there they gathered more names for the enterprise. Roberts picked up on their interest and introduced them to Oxford University student Glenn Nesbitt, who in turn mentioned another Oxford student Michael McClenahan. Along the way, with David Jackman's prompting, they made contact with Oak Hill College north of central London. From these references, a stable of young British writers was enlisted, including Matthew Mason, Nick Tucker, and Mark O'Donoghue.

Capitol Hill Baptist Church's pastor, Mark Dever, was also a help in this connection. He had a DPhil in ecclesiastical history from Cambridge, and a variety of friends in the UK, some of whom contacted with him from time to time in Washington. (Indeed, the aforementioned Vaughan Roberts met Doug Baker in Dever's study, when Roberts was visiting his sister in Virginia.)

On that same UK trip, Doug Baker and Pastor Bob were able to visit the Bunhill Fields cemetery, the final resting place for several notables, including Daniel Defoe, who wrote Robinson Crusoe; Susannah Wesley, mother of John and Charles; and poet William Blake. Baker and Phillips were particularly interested in visiting the final resting places of John Bunyan (*Pilgrim's Progress*) and Isaac Watts (*Joy to the World; When I Survey the Wondrous Cross*), and there they teared up as they prayed God would similarly guide and empower their efforts.

Blessing Young Scholar/Writers

Once back in the US, the Kampourises and Doug (again, whom you'll meet more fully in the next chapter) began building an invitation list for a series of writers camps in Washington, DC, now with fresh British names in the mix. None of us had taken part in such a tryout, one in which there were no losers, since it involved an all-expenses-paid-plus-stipend trip to the nation's capital, replete with collegial fellowship, edifying study, thoughtful conversation, and a banquet with exposure to luminaries. At first blush, it seemed too good to be true. (As Glenn Nesbitt recalls, "I put down the phone and wondered to myself if this was all a joke.")

Of course, once the team selections were made, and we were up and running, the experience of writing and editing together continued to be gratifying. As Nesbitt (now a senior lecturer at Johannesburg Bible College) put it (for all of us):

> I valued the opportunity to write a few of those articles, especially the historical ones. I appreciated the discipline of composing one A4 page [8.27 x 11.7", the international counterpart to the US 8.5 x 11"], of making it punchy and readable and of having to stick to a template [which Mr. K had imposed to ensure discipline]. My ability to express myself improved greatly and I enjoyed having to think about and research topics I had given little consideration to.

Another of the Brits, Nick Tucker, recalls, "Mr. K's gentle, humble, yet highly impressive leadership set the tone for all the *KJ* meetings I was part of. It was a privilege for me to see the way that for all his gifts and his successes, Mr. K's predominant mien was a Christlike humility and servant heartedness."

In that vein, Michael McClennahan (now a professor of systematic theology at Union Theological College in Belfast) comments on "Mr. Kampouris's ability to listen carefully to a long and complex discussion and then enter it just at the right moment to sum up the problem—and ask for a solution!" He also notes Mr. K's "ability in meetings to draw out those who were not speaking but whom he knew had something to contribute."

Of course, the tone of the meeting was occasionally tense as we took turns rating one another's contributions or sorting out what we would count as "kosher" or not. (As Glenn Nesbitt put it, "Our editorial meetings were bruising at times and yet filled with grace.") And there was a lot of laughter, with Nick supplying us his share. He'd written a piece on Isaiah 56:10-12, one critical of church leaders who fit the bill as "blind watchmen," "silent watchdogs," and "shepherds without understanding." It began with this apocryphal (but popular on the Internet) newspaper report:

> "We will not have him put down. Lucky is basically a good guide dog," Ernst Gerber, a dog trainer from Wuppertal told reporters. Gerber admitted that Lucky, a guide dog for the blind, had so far been responsible for the deaths of all four of his previous owners. "He led his first owner in front of a moving bus, and the second off the end of a pier. He actually pushed the third owner off a railway platform just as the Cologne to Frankfurt express was approaching, and he walked his fourth owner into heavy traffic before abandoning him and running away to safety. But apart from the epileptic fits, he has a

lovely temperament. And guide dogs are difficult to train these days."

Under the hand of Greg Thornbury, "Lucky" morphed into a history piece and then into a current-trends article naming names. Alas, in the end, it failed to make the cut since one of the team judged the wound to be counter-productively deep and too close for comfort in his neck of the woods. Still, upon each reading of yet another iteration (on February 8, 2003, August 5, 2003, and June 3, 2004), we got a great kick out of it.

Though the journal itself was the point to this ministry, the ancillary benefits to budding ministers—the "scholarship" system, if you will—was substantial. Nick Tucker (now the vicar of St. Bartholomew's Edgbaston in Birmingham, England) writes,

> Mr. K came into my life in a rather miraculous way that completely changed my future. I was looking to take on master's studies at the end of my seminary training at Oak Hill College, but disaster had struck. There is a system for funding postgrad studies within the Church of England, and I had been progressing through the process well, when suddenly (for various disappointing reasons that I won't rehearse here) I hit a brick wall; funding was denied and it seemed very unlikely that I would be able to continue. My tutor at the time, Mike Ovey [whom we'll meet later in Nairobi] reassured me that "if God wants you to do this it will happen," and I thought to myself, "Well, I guess he just doesn't want me to do this then."
>
> The same week, Matthew Mason, who had been one of the first Brits involved with *KJ*, mentioned that they might just be looking for a couple more writers from the UK. Within a month or two, I found

> myself onboard the good ship *KJ*, and, due to Mr. K's generosity, able to take on the course of study that it turns out God did want me to take after all.

And it wasn't just the stipend. Mr. K became a career shaper for Nick, as well.

> My first conversation with Mr. K on a transatlantic line as he was considering whether or not to add me to the writers team, was also very influential on me. I felt pretty confident in being able to write some biblical pieces for *KJ* and felt very deskilled in other areas. But Mr. K, in his gentle but apparently irresistible way, explained to me that I could write history. This was something I certainly doubted, but he apparently knew better, and to my astonishment, he turned out to be right. A few years later I was teaching church history at Oak Hill and writing a PhD on the subject.

(Nick's "audition piece" was a fairly arcane disquisition on theology, and he might have been excused from the group, but Mr. K noticed he was a rugby player, and so gave him further consideration, which proved prescient.)

Glenn Nesbitt adds his version of critical assistance:

> Working for the Journal enabled me to pay my theological college fees and other expenses. In fact, by the time of our wedding, it was the one job I had, so on our marriage certificate it states my occupation as a writer!

And, of course, "Amens" come from across the pond, as this one from Shane Walker (now the senior pastor of Andover Baptist Church in Linthicum, Maryland):

I was studying political philosophy several years before I met Mr. K. Advancing my education had been stymied by lack of funds and leisure time. As I read yet another philosopher, poet, or theologian thanking his patron for allowing him the time and funds to study, I turned to God in prayer and requested a patron. As far as I can tell, God brought me to *KJ* in answer to that prayer.

On top of this, the Brits enjoyed the travel and tourism that *KJ* provided. Glenn Nesbitt remembers:

I have admired the US ever since I was a child so to finally visit Washington, DC and New York were dreams come true. I loved the four weeks I spent in DC in July/August 2002 and it remains one of my favorite places. In evenings, after I had finished writing, I would walk down the Mall to the monuments and soak up the atmosphere. I have promised my wife I will take her there one day, and hopefully also to NYC. The fact that *KJ* facilitated those visits and that they involved writing and the team made them even more memorable.

And it wasn't just the monuments that caught their attention, but also the local color. In this connection, Nick mentions a New York cabbie, and a follow-up experience his last night in Manhattan on his first visit.

A few days earlier, the five of us from the UK had arrived in this magnificent city and had the first evening free. We had found something to eat and were walking back to our hotel when we came upon a yellow cab that had got stuck behind another car. The cab driver was leaning out of his window, gesticulating wildly with the hand that he was not using to lean on his horn and yelling, "Wadda you doin' you mawrahn," at the top of his lungs in a voice that sounded just like every New York cabbie we had ever heard in a movie. We were highly impressed, and it took an effort of the will for us to refrain from applauding. We, of course, told everyone who would listen about this encounter, including Mr. K. On the last night of that trip, after a delicious meal at a nearby restaurant, we were once again walking back to our hotel, when a car horn blared to our right and a man was leaning out of a moving car shouting at us, "What are you boys doing?" It was Mr. K. He had remembered our story and was re-enacting it for us (though much more politely and with rather more finesses) as a fond farewell to Manhattan.

The Marnhams were also well engaged with the work in America. They attended board meetings in New York twice a year and took part in some of the "round the table" editorial discussions, coming away "from those meetings energized and inspired." They marveled at "how Mano looked for excellence in everything—from the gifted writers and theologians he had assembled to his great attention to detail." They also prized the way Mano and Camille worked as a team and bathed everything in prayer: "Even when a project might hit a rocky patch, as some did, they were always content to leave it in God's hands, knowing that in His time, He would work things out." Like the others who've spoken, they were struck by the Kampouris's "amazing generosity, kindness, and practical care." (Along the way, they learned that while at American Standard, Mano had brought in dieticians to lecture the work force on healthy living—and to this day, Charles and Tricia try to have berries for breakfast as Mano and Camille do.)

The *KJ* Way

Though the source is unclear (with many attributing the quote to George Bernard Shaw), it's said that England and America are "two nations separated by a common language." As managing editor of *Kairos Journal*, I didn't find this to be the case, but, in my work, I did find us often separated by punctuation and spelling. Clinging to my *Chicago Manual of Style*, I moved closing quotation marks outside the period and added a period after 'Mr.' Also, I found the British more comma-averse than the average American, and I had to pull the 'u' out of 'colour' and 'humour.' Still, not much trouble—and, of course, it was arbitrary. (For what it's worth, I think the quotation marks work better inside the period.)

Things did get interesting on a few matters of substance. When I was at Oak Hill for a little workshop with our UK crew on "the *KJ* way," we found ourselves diverging on questions of church and state. As a Baptist from America, I was more of a separationist (though not an extreme one) than my British website colleagues. America had a First Amendment, with a no-establishment clause, and England did not. Furthermore, several of them were in studies for the priesthood in the established Anglican Church.

Then there was the dustup over Augustine, the first archbishop of Canterbury (not the Augustine who wrote *Confessions* and *City of God*). I'd done an amiable piece on this man credited with introducing Christianity to England, and at the first group reading, an Ulster Presbyterian expressed his great lack of enthusiasm for this Catholic (Benedictine) agent of Rome. He'd arrived around AD 600, and it wasn't until the sixteenth century that the post turned Anglican. Still, we proved right adept at sorting things out. As Peter Riddell (who joined our team while Director of the Centre for Islamic Studies and Muslim-Christian Relations at London School of Theology) puts it:

> The complementary nature of the team is quite re-
> markable. Each member brings specific skills and
> experience to the table, and those pieces then fit to-
> gether like a puzzle to form a coherent whole. Being
> part of the *KJ* team is extremely satisfying because
> individual members receive respect for their own

> contributions, while at the same time having the
> opportunity to learn vast amounts of information
> from other members.

And so, it was iron sharpening iron—parts of the body functioning in concert.

Marnham at the Hay-Adams

Closing out this chapter, I'll return to Charles Marnham, who was asked to speak at the first of six writers-camp dinners at the Hay-Adams Hotel on July 18, 2002. In his address, "For Such a Time as This," he began by quoting the bishop of Rochester, who just two weeks earlier, before the General Synod of the Church of England, said the church was "facing a time of exile as its influence in the country [had] waned. Many [believed] that Christianity [was] rapidly becoming invisible and the Christian voice [was] increasingly ignored." He added that Cardinal Cormac Murphy-O'Connor, head of the English and Welsh Roman Catholics, had declared that "Christianity had been all but vanquished when it came to influencing public policy."

Charles then listed a number of signs that a hostile and relativistic secularism was ascendant. Among those was the power the Mystical and Occult Foundation enjoyed in bullying a Christian radio station over its biblical stance on homosexuality, and also the fact that adult church attendance in Great Britain had dropped by more than a million from 1980 to 2000. ("By 2000, only 8 percent of the population attended church, and we are talking attendance—not necessarily commitment.") And those who came to church weren't necessarily given what they needed. As Australia's Philip Jensen put it, it was as if the clergy were saying, "You're heading towards a huge crash, but it is all right because you're driving along very nicely." What the people needed to hear was, "You're going the wrong way—turn 'round now!"

Charles declared:

> I believe that if church leaders are going to regain
> their God-given role in society, then they must start
> with this biblical model; unashamed of the gospel;
> utterly confident in the transforming power of the
> Word of God; unafraid to speak out and be called a
> fool or a maniac; even to be unpopular with other
> religious leaders; deeply aware of their accountabil-
> ity to God if they do not speak out. And sharing
> God's longing that people would turn back to Him.

He expressed the hope that pastors would become "practitioner
watchmen," and he gave thanks to the Kampouris's team: "You are
providing a research assistant of the highest caliber for potentially
every minister throughout the world." He closed by quoting a prayer
Joe Wright, a Kansas pastor, delivered before the state senate. Some
legislators walked out, but thousands called in support. Charles commended Wright's convictions and courage to us as we began our
work on *Kairos Journal*:

> Heavenly Father we ask Your forgiveness. We know
> your Word says, "Woe on those who call evil good,"
> but that's exactly what we have done and we confess
> that:
>
> We have ridiculed the absolute truth of Your Word
> and called it pluralism.
> We have endorsed perversion and called it an alter-
> native lifestyle.
> We have exploited the poor and called it the lottery.
> We have neglected the needy and called it
> self-preservation.
> We have killed our unborn children and called it
> choice.

We have neglected to discipline our children and called it self-expression.

We have abused power and called it political savvy.

We have coveted our neighbor's possessions and called it ambition.

We have polluted the air with profanity and pornography and called it freedom of expression.

We have ridiculed the time-honored values of our forefathers and called it enlightenment.

Search us, O God, know our hearts today; cleanse us from every sin and set us free in the Name of Your Son, the Living Savior, Jesus Christ. Amen.

And all the *KJ* people said, "Amen!"

Camille and Mano, wed in 1992

Kampourises: Andrew and Sarah, Emmanuel and Camille, Ivey and Alexander

Emmanuel and Elena Kampouris (children of Alexander and Ivey) at
Elena's opening night in *Les Liaisons Dangereuses* on Broadway,
where she played Cecile, opposite Liev Schreiber

Timothy, Madeleine, and Myrto Kampouris (children of Andrew and Sarah)

On break from a hotel work session: (l to r, front row) Michael McClenahan, Doug Baker, Bob Phillips, Emmanuel Kampouris, Camille Kampouris, Glenn Nesbitt, Mark O'Donoghue, Nick Tucker (l to r, back row) Greg Thornbury, Shane Walker, Matthew Mason, Brian Pinney, Greg Gilbert, Brad Green, Dimitri Kampouris, Mark Coppenger, Ben Mitchell

Kairos Journal editing session at the Kampouris's Manhattan apartment: (l to r) Mark Coppenger, Aaron Menikoff, Charles Marnham, Brian Pinney, Camille Kampouris, Emmanuel Kampouris, and Jacob Shatzer (Photo by Tricia Marnham.)

The Kampourises with the four Anglican archbishops honored by the 2005 *Kairos Journal* Award: (l to r) Henry Orombi, Peter Akinola, Datuk Yong Ping Chung, Gregory Venables

Swedish pastor Aake Green, with his translator, meeting with the team in New York

Daniel Scot (of Pakistan and Australia), recipient of the 2007 *Kairos Journal* Award

Peter Riddell scans a newspaper for items of interest to
Kairos Journal (Photo by Tricia Marnham.)

Tricia Marnham in a video introducing the Biblical Story course on BibleMesh

BibleMesh Biblical Languages booth at the Society for Biblical Literature meeting, with Greek editor, Mark Dubis of Union University, speaking to visitors

CHAPTER 13

"I Need a Guy Who Knows Politics and Theology."
(Building a Team of Yanks)

Keen to raise up John Venns so they might encourage William Wilberforces, the Kampourises began searching for a man who could help them get underway. They spoke to Kenneth O'Connor, president of the Family Research Council (FRC) in Washington, DC, and Alan Crippen of the Witherspoon Institute. They wondered if they knew a fellow who knew politics and theology, and the name Doug Baker surfaced. He'd earned a master of divinity degree (MDiv) at New Orleans Baptist Theological Seminary and had been a speech writer for Arkansas Governor Mike Huckabee for a couple of years.

Mano invited him to New York to talk with him and Camille and Bob Phillips. Doug had never been to the city, and he recalls it was "country comes to town." He thought this was a courtesy visit, one in which he'd pitch in on the notion of a website with political and theological orientation. He thought it would be a "one-off" meeting, one in which he'd serve as a resource.

Baker and the Kampourises clicked from the start, agreeing, for instance, on the primacy of the local church (in the spirit of Mark Dever, Ligon Duncan, and Albert Mohler); sharing an appreciation for William Wilberforce and Charles Simeon, convinced of the Bible's application to all of culture; and agreeing with Daniel Patrick Moynihan that "politics was downstream from culture." Mano was well ahead of Doug in his grasp of websites and his enthusiasm was infectious. Doug later reflected, "Mr. K had a way of seeing the future and getting there first." He came to see that the Kampourises were very quick studies: "You could give them thirty days and they'd go toe to toe on any topic." As for the projected website, with its quadrants and historical sweep, Baker added, "I'd never seen someone's mind work that way, thinking so comprehensively, moving from parts to the whole and back again."

Back in DC, Baker was surprised to get a call from O'Connor saying the Kampourises would like to hire him and that he should give them a call. Indeed, they were serious and eager to start. They wanted to draw on his ability to "put the brakes on hermeneutics" where needed, in the mold of Carl F. H. Henry, and they wanted him to get going right away in assembling writers from around the country, which he did. Though Doug was going to work full time for the Kampourises, FRC was happy to provide him an office from which to work.

Brian Pinney

The first order of business was to get an assistant to help with what was proving to be a substantial enterprise. By God's grace, he found just the man in Brian Pinney—by Doug's account, one who "executed details perfectly; studious in theology; a trusted advisor and hard worker; able to see strategically; able to take a small germ of an idea and flesh it out; the *sine qua non* of *Kairos Journal*."

Brian was a product of Toccoa, Georgia, where his father, David Flederjohann, was employed at the local Christian college, Toccoa Falls. The night of November 6, 1977, after knocking on doors to warn residents of the danger of the dam collapsing upstream, David was tragically killed by the 30 ft. high wall of water which breached the dam. God was gracious to provide for the family, and Brian pressed ahead with life (as a Pinney, taking his stepfather's surname).

He went on to take a degree at the college, focusing on U.S. history and secondary education. As a first-year public school teacher (teaching subjects outside his field, namely psychology and sociology), he was burning the candle at both ends. He was also working on a master's degree and pursuing a serious long-distance relationship, thus getting few hours of sleep at night. He became burned out on teaching and suffered from depression, even entertaining thoughts of suicide. His doctor suggested he should find employment at physical jobs, so he started working for a construction company (wanting to learn how to build a house). He worked his way up to becoming an assistant foreman.

From there, he completed a master's degree in teaching and returned to the classroom. But, he decided he didn't want to do that for the remainder of his life. He soon applied for a Witherspoon Fellowship in public theology at the FRC, where his brother served. Through it, he came to DC in the wake of 9/11.

As his semester-long internship was coming to an end, Brian had to decide what came next. God had healed his mind enough to return to teaching or maybe attend seminary. The latter option grew on him along with the conviction that the emphasis on natural law and reason (the focus of his program at Witherspoon) left much to be said when it came to the biblical and spiritual aspects of turning hearts and minds. Reformed Theological Seminary had a DC extension and it seemed a good fit, so he set himself on that track with a look toward selling Cutco knives for financial support.

Then, Doug Baker stepped in.

Brian was rooming with John Ranheim, to whom Doug had offered the job of assistant, but Ranheim stayed on the path which would take him to Covenant College as director of advancement. Brian's name was also in the mix, and, with a recommendation from Alan Crippen, Doug offered him the job, which he accepted. In that connection, both Doug and Brian kept offices at FRC (with Brian performing other duties in house) before they moved their work to an apartment office in Arlington, Virginia, in the summer of 2002.

Doug Baker, Hunter/Gatherer

Mr. K was solicitous of Doug and eager to help him, in a fatherly way, to step up his game. For instance, Doug had a green Chevy Lumina, one Mr. K judged to be "the ugliest car I've ever seen." So he helped him get a new Nissan Maxima, and urged him to be careful (for he knew how fast Doug drove). Sure enough, the second day Doug had the car, a policeman pulled him over for driving 55 mph in a 45-mph zone near the Pentagon. At that very moment, Mr. K called and asked, "Where are you?" "I'm at work ... I'm getting a ticket." "I told you! You're going to pay that ticket, young man!"

In assembling writers, Doug began with Greg Thornbury, at the time a Union University professor of philosophy and religion. Greg in turn approached his faculty colleague, Brad Green, and a network of gifted young evangelicals who'd been his students at Union. In due course, a number of them came on board. They included Jacob Shatzer, who went on to earn the MDiv at SBTS and the PhD at Marquette, and who now teaches at his alma mater, Union, and Matthew Crawford, who also earned the MDiv at Southern and is now a research fellow at the Catholic University of Australia in Melbourne, having earned the PhD at Durham University. (Doug also pitched my name into the mix, for which I'm eternally grateful.)

Mark Dever, pastor of Capitol Hill Baptist Church, was another help in building the team. Indeed, in the summer of 2002, CHBC hosted the six aforementioned writers camps, with a succession of candidates staying in a B&B across the street and enjoying access to the Library of Congress. Dever suggested names from his own congregation, some of them pastoral interns, such as Greg Gilbert, a Yale graduate in the MDiv program at SBTS who now pastors Third Avenue Baptist Church in Louisville and has penned some books for Crossway under their IX Marks imprint; Aaron Menikoff, with a bachelor of arts degree from Oregon and a PhD from SBTS, now pastor of Mount Vernon Baptist Church in Atlanta; and Shane Walker (whom we met in the previous chapter), with a bachelor of arts degree from Iowa and an MDiv from SBTS, now pastor of Andover Baptist Church in the Baltimore area.

(Through the years, a wide range of other writers were invited to pitch in—Paul Gavrilyuk of the University of St. Thomas in St. Paul, Minnesota; George Kalantzis, then of Garrett Evangelical Seminary, now of Wheaton College; Peter Richards, who'd taught Constitutional Law at the U.S. Air Force Academy; Jeremy Pierre of SBTS; and pastors, such as Greg's father, John Thornbury of Winfield Baptist Church in Winfield, Pennsylvania; Stan Wiedeman of Lakeside Church in Skokie, Illinois; Phil Newton of South Woods Baptist Church in Memphis, Tennessee; and Richard Stratton of First Baptist Church, Hendersonville, Kentucky.)

Each day, the "campers" met for updates and then split up to tackle writing assignments, submitted by close of day to Doug Baker, the Kampourises, and Bob Phillips, who was now pastor of Encourager Church in Houston. One evening each week, the group gathered for dinner at the Hay-Adams Hotel, with a visiting speaker (for example, Congressman J. C. Watts and U.S. Ambassador-at-Large for International Religious Freedom John Hanford), who'd address some aspect of Christian impact in the public square.

Both Greg and Doug had the impression that Ben Mitchell (MDiv, Southwestern Baptist Theological Seminary; PhD, Tennessee) was important to the enterprise, and he was duly recruited. As professor of bioethics at Trinity Evangelical Divinity School, he added expertise in a variety of topics the journal would address such as stem cell research, reproductive technologies, and euthanasia. On a visit to Trinity, Greg took a *Kairos Journal* flip-chart book by Ben's office, giving him a look at the project and saying, "We need someone to write on life issues." Ben showed interest, and before he knew it, the Kampouris's travel agent (who worked with Camille at Ichabod's and who has artfully "herded cats," arranging countless trips and stays for us, in and to and from all corners of the globe) had booked him in and out of New York for a meeting. He thought, "Nobody with these resources can be this interested in the church. And they want to give things to pastors?!" Well, indeed they were ... and they did. And Ben was on board.

Looking back, Ben's wife Nancy says it reminded her of patrons who, centuries ago, had ministers on call to teach their children. We've sometimes reflected on the way in which we were something of a mini-seminary for the Kampourises. They were strong in entrepreneurial, administrative, and cultural arts. We brought them the fruit of biblical studies, church history, apologetics, and pastoral ministry. (Of course, they were widely read, and Mano could run circles around us in Greek. And, of course, we'd had a variety of experiences beyond the groves of academe. But we're talking centers of mass here.)

Operational Tempo

Once the team was set, with personnel selections from among the camp participants, we began the project in earnest, with frequent visits to the Kampouris's apartment in New York City and their home near Morristown, New Jersey. I was tapped as managing editor, and armed with the *Chicago Manual of Style*, I got to work.

As often as once a month, a half dozen of us flew to the East Coast for marathon editing sessions, some covering nearly fifty articles submitted in advance. (Brian supplied us with "Gap Analysis" sheets to help show us "who'd been naughty and who'd been nice" in terms of output.) Typically, we'd begin at 9:00 a.m., and work, with a short break, until lunch on site or out in their Manhattan neighborhood, and then pick up again in an hour, going until around 7:00 p.m., finally breaking to assemble for dinner at a great restaurant about a half hour later. (In between these trips, we'd meet frequently by phone, the longest session running five hours, after which I decided to buy a headset to save me the pain of holding a receiver to my ear for so long.)

We marveled at the Ks, in that they seemed to get stronger the later we went in the day. As we writers were sinking around 4:30 p.m., they seemed to enjoy a burst of energy, and, were it not for dinner reservations, we might have gone on until midnight. Furthermore, dinner wasn't just a quick bite before bed, but rather a two-hour affair with a succession of courses and conversations. I think it was a European thing, something that didn't come so naturally for us Yanks who were used to sixish suppers, wrapped up no later than 7:00 p.m. It was, in the final analysis, grand and a privilege.

And their generosity was flabbergasting, as we found ourselves enjoying meals three and four times the cost of what was ordinarily for us a fine evening of dining. We became, to our astonishment, habituated to eating at such neighborhood establishments as Rothmann's, Bice, Michael's, Milos, and Chat Noir. It was all that us seminary students, church planters, and junior professors could handle.

Indeed, the operational tempo was heavy in the early going, with monthly trips to the East Coast. (These gave way to quarterly gatherings as we settled into our routines.) But I should mention January 2003, when we were scrambling to make a strong start. Looking back through my journals, I read that it was a two-trip month, once to their home in New Jersey, the other to their Manhattan apartment. On January 7-8, we worked through about fifty pieces; from January 17-19, we tackled another forty articles submitted by our writers (and by us editors). On that second trip, we spent time with two Brits, Charley Hoare (the UN representative for CARE) and Paul Diamond (a barrister who briefed us on Christian liberty cases in England).

That same month, when not in New York, we had conference calls on six separate days, the calls typically running about three hours. For example, we handled nineteen pieces on January 22, between 2:30 and 5:15 p.m., and then another twenty-five or so on January 27 between 3:00 and 6:00 p.m. I note that nine of the articles were essentially good to go, cleared for final cleanup or posting. (We joined these calls from ever-changing venues; sometimes the Ks signed in from London or Bermuda; Michael McClenahan might be doing some work stateside at Yale in connection with his Oxford doctorate; Brian might be at his home in Dayton or on the road down south visiting relatives; once I "dialed in" from Borneo, another time from a ship in Alaskan waters.)

Each week I sent a summary of our progress to all the writers and did my own writing and editing almost daily. I developed an original piece called "Strangers in the World" on I Peter on January 2 and "The Abortionist as 'Bible Scholar'"—drawing from Exodus 21—on January 22. (Incidentally, that was the same day Sharon and I shared our 32nd wedding anniversary, with flowers arriving from "The *KJ* Team.")

In addition to joining the group calls, I found myself in a variety of one-on-ones, including an email exchange with Doug Baker about natural law; a phone call with Brad Green about a Zechariah article; and a Kairos-topics conversation with Ben Mitchell, not far up the North Shore from Evanston. And, of course, there was research, as when I ran by the Evanston library to get a book on Margaret Sanger (for "Margaret Sanger: Enabling a 'Liberated' Woman"). The days were exhilarating, challenging, and a little exhausting. And the Kampourises were in on every minute, following every line we wrote.

Hospitality

Whether we met at the home in New Jersey or their apartment in Manhattan, we got the best treatment from the Kampouris's employees—Elizabeth Martinez in New Jersey, who was particularly cherished for the cookies she made us for Christmas; Mauricio Balter in New York, who kept us well supplied with coffee, tea, and a variety of nuts, some of them chocolate-covered (not the best thing for sedentary days, but worth the pain of subsequent dieting); Gail Dalais and

Rose Beth Mickel, who handled our chaotic bundles of receipts for reimbursement with ingenuity and patience; and then there was the driver, Ron Skobo, whose service we appreciatively/anxiously called "Air Ron" for the way he'd speed us to our flights at Newark. He had an FBI background, and I know he could teach evasive driving for corporate chauffeurs—the sort of guy you'd want behind the wheel if you were being chased by terrorists on the back streets of Mogadishu.

One evening, the Kampourises were finishing up some matter, and they sent me ahead with a crew of six or seven writers to Rothmann's with the credit card. They figured they could trust my judgment. They were wrong. When I looked at the appetizers on the menu, I saw some sort of seafood extravaganza for (as I recall) around $40. It seemed like a good idea, but then, when we were into it, I discovered that the ziggurat of shrimp, crab legs, etc., was $40 a person, thus bringing the appetizer alone to around $250. I apologized profusely, and, mercifully, my wages were not garnished. The Kampourises chalked it up to a provincial's mistake.

The Boiler Room

The editing sessions were alternately stirring, stupefying, edifying, and brutal. One person, often the author, would read a piece to the crew gathered around the big dining room table at the Manhattan apartment, and then anyone and everyone weighed in. Camille and Mano, in particular, insisted upon accessibility in language, on putting the cookies on the bottom shelf. (That's not to say Camille demanded *Sesame Street* vocabulary; she was Phi Beta Kappa from CUA and an accomplished communicator at every reasonable level.) On this model, you'd better not deploy 'eleemosynary' when 'charitable' would work just fine.

To help keep us concise, Mr. K gave us subscriptions to *The Economist* to underscore the point that you could say pretty much what you needed to say on a single page. Our version of that one-page rule meant "standard margins, 11-point, *Times New Roman*, excepting footnotes," which often ran well into the second page. Shane Walker remembers some counsel we got in this connection:

> We were at an editorial meeting when Mr. K announced that he had counted all the words in Stephen's speech in Acts, and that, in less than 500 words, Stephen had covered all of salvation history, presented a legal argument in defense of preaching the gospel, and had a vision. He then told us to stop whining about the length of articles at *KJ*.

Though we professors were inclined to supply them already, Mr. K made sure to press us for careful research and painstaking documentation. This isn't to say hard work always paid off in group approval. As Shane Walker recalls in connection with a day of research in the Library of Congress:

> At one point either Doug Baker or someone else required that I transcribe sermons from the Rump Parliament from about 1648. (My memory is that someone thought they would be helpful sermons.) The things only existed in the special collections room as pamphlets. To gain access you had to prove to the librarians that you didn't have ink pens, and they took away your book bags. Then, when the librarians would bring out the sermons, I was required to place the pamphlet on a velvet covered wedge using velvet covered lead weights to hold the papers back. The paper was so dry that I could feel it dehydrate my fingertips when I touched it.
>
> I spent something near two days working out orthography issues, dealing with lacuna, and typing terrifyingly slowly. When I finally staggered out with a couple complete sermons as a Word document, Mrs. K was horrified, because the sermons

were miserable. (I still remember her face; it was like I had brought her a dead cat.) Bizarro stuff, apocalyptic and so contemporaneous as to be completely worthless for modern audiences and likely not so edifying when preached. Even so, I was honored just to be allowed to touch documents that old.

Three of the *Journal*'s four quadrants followed a strict template. The biblical pieces began with the Scripture in italics, followed by at least a paragraph on each of the items of our LCAC template—Lead; Commentary; Application; Call to Action. The historical articles fell out as EPNL—Introductory Event; Periodization; Narrative; Lesson. And then, when we featured quotations in quadrant three, we introduced each with DPPP—Date; Historical Period; the Person; the Point. The fourth quadrant, featuring "contemporary trends" with editorial comment, was more free form. But all had to fall within a page. (I supply annotated samples of the four approaches as appendices.)

The Reach

When all was said and done, we'd approved and posted more than 2,400 articles, many of them translated into seven different languages—French, Greek, Russian, Spanish, Portuguese, Mandarin, and Simplified Chinese (with Arabic in the works).

Today, more than ten thousand ministers, spread out within one hundred different nations, have registered to read them. (We limited registration to ministers for several reasons—to underscore our special esteem for their strategic role; to keep us on message to this select group; to provide them fresh illustrative material not likely familiar to their parishioners; and to protect them from aggressive members who might use our "calls to action" as cudgels to abuse the ministers who'd not yet answered those calls). Now, they're open to all who purchase the Thomas Nelson *Unapologetic Study Bible*, which incorporates more than four hundred of the journal's articles.

Mark Coppenger

The Research

We built the *Kairos Journal* corpus over an eight-year period, and those of us involved in the process felt as though we'd earned another seminary degree. (In Jacob Shatzer's words, "The men and women I worked with on *Kairos Journal* impacted me as much if not more than the faculty I worked with in seminary and graduate school.") Each time we met, we came away with gratitude for a newly-discovered historical hero, a new concept, etc. And those of us bringing these items to the fold were pretty excited to make the introduction. I remember, for instance, how much fun it was to present a draft piece on Nonie Darwish (a convert from Islam to Christianity, who founded Arabs for Israel) and Gerardo, the "Brother of Faith" (who preached faithfully in Castro's Isle of Pines prison).

Greg Thornbury remembers how much he enjoyed getting better acquainted with the life and work of British Prime Minister William Gladstone and how his study led him to fourth-century Bishop Hosius of Cordova. Hosius had been a stalwart along with Athanasius at the Council of Nicaea against the Arian heresy (that Jesus was the first of God's creation and not himself co-eternal with the Father), but late in life the heretics rose to power and mistreated him. He was transferred to a minor post in modern-day Croatia and endured a range of pressures, indignities, and even tortures for his stand. Finally, he recanted and was allowed to live out his days comfortably back in Spain. It's a sad but compelling story—the spectacle of a minister not finishing well. And *Kairos Journal* gave Greg the opportunity to dig into his story, a privilege we all experienced as we discovered our own Hosiuses. In turn, we "met" the Bulgarian Orthodox bishops who defended their nation's Jews during the Holocaust; the nineteenth-century missionary to Muslims, Henry Martyn; Pliny the Younger, whose first-century, outsider description of Christians honored the early church; and the second century's Athenagoras, who condemned abortion.

To stir the pot, the Ks often flew in seminal Christian thinkers to spend the morning or day with us—luminaries such as Os Guinness, Frederica Mathewes-Green, Peter Harris, and William Abraham.

Grateful Reflections

Reflecting on the *Kairos* experience, Thornbury said the Kampourises were exemplary for:

1. Their "thick ecumenism" … "for though most of the writers were Reformed-minded Baptists and Presbyterians, there were frequent contributions from those in the Anglican, Orthodox, and Catholic traditions." (In this vein, Shatzer reported, "The *KJ* team was my first exposure to classic evangelicalism, with folks from various traditions working diligently and joyfully together on common kingdom work.")

2. Their interest in world Christianity before people were talking about the Global South. (In this connection, they gave out awards and invited people well outside their own denominational bubbles).

3. Their radical commitment to Carl F. H. Henry's view that the Bible addressed everything—law, economics, politics, science, etc.

"And they put their money where their mouth was."

Thornbury credits the experience with making him a more disciplined writer, and, by his account, it "took the edge off his cockiness," for that "just wouldn't fly in our group," where "nobody was better than another." The operation was "very egalitarian, a Christlike thing," reminiscent of Jesus' choice of fishermen rather than dignitaries from the rabbinic school.

All of us understood we were privileged to be in the mix, for we knew we weren't that impressive. As Greg puts it, "Mano and Camille were willing to work with the B-Squad, and all of us were afraid that 'the fraud police would show up.'" And Shane Walker recalls, "At one point in a *KJ* meeting, I was sitting in a room with, I believe, two Anglican archbishops from Africa, important Baptists, Methodists, and Presbyterian dignitaries, and a Greek Orthodox bishop."

Indeed, we all felt privileged to be in the mix. Greg Gilbert called the opportunity "huge." He was headed to Southern for the MDiv, and the Gilberts were counting on income from his wife Moriah's work to sustain them. But then she got pregnant, and he needed a job. Kairos brought all the pieces together, providing "incredible support," and giving him engaging work until President Al Mohler brought him on full-time as his assistant.

Greg recalls the editorial meetings as "hugely inefficient," but that was right to the point of the fellowship of minds and mutual education the team, and especially the Kampourises, enjoyed. And, along the way, he picked up a number of articles on homosexuality, and someone nicknamed him the "Gay Czar." I (with military background—twenty-eight years in the Army National Guard and Reserves as an infantry officer) tackled most of the articles on armed conflict and so became the "War Czar."

Aaron Menikoff, a writer from 2003 to 2008, also has rich memories of our time together.

> In God's providence, this writing assignment came at the perfect time. I had finished my MDiv and was starting a doctorate in church history. My family had begun to grow—we had just had our second child. The prospect of another five years in school was daunting. Making ends meet so that Deana could be with the kids as much as possible wouldn't be easy.

I got a phone call that seemed out of the blue ...
I learned later that Mark Dever had reached out
to someone in the Kairos camp (I think Greg T.)
to have them take a look at me. God provided me
the dream job: I got to research and write and talk
through some of the greatest challenges facing the
church with some of the most humble folks around.

1. Mrs. Kampouris is thoughtful and serious. No
    formal theological training that I was aware of
    and yet happy to go toe-to-toe with any scholar
    when it came to helping a piece serve the church.
    She expressed such care for the writers—con-
    cerned about us being comfortable, healthy.
    Like an older sister looking out for the younger
    ones. She prized everyone working together as
    a team.

2. Mr. Kampouris. I couldn't understand why we
    had a section on bribery. What was I supposed to
    write on the topic of bribery that would be help-
    ful to churches? Is this really an issue? I asked
    this question more than once. I figured it was a
    particular interest of his since he had served his
    whole life in the business world, but as a PhD
    student it wasn't obvious to me. Nonetheless, I
    sought to provide as many pieces on the topic
    as I could. A few years later, I became a pastor
    at a church in Atlanta. Imagine my surprise to
    discover that bribery is a real issue regularly
    faced by Christians in the business world!

3. The editorial team they put together led through
    encouragement. Pieces were edited without
    sympathy for the author. But I always believed
    the team had my back and wanted me in the

room. Nobody made me feel out of place. They encouraged so much that when it came time for a piece to be axed, I couldn't take it personally. There was no need to. There was a sense of love on the team.

4. Writing for the team was fun. The group cared about theology, ethics, and the church. And they laughed while doing it. Greg T. pacing the dining room and introducing us to Union's latest campus social media environment—assuring us it would be the next "big thing." Mark C. telling us how he liked to read everything and anything—it was all interesting, he said, even grain reports from the Midwest. Mrs. K scolding us for eating too much chocolate.

Looking back, I'm sure Kairos did much more for me than I did for it. It exposed me to an evangelical world much larger than the one I had seen at a Southern Baptist seminary. It taught me about the pains of the persecuted church and the need for a robust engagement with an Islamic worldview. It drastically improved my writing, helping me to make simple points with a punch. It put food on the table, allowing me to finish my degree so that I could soon devote my life to serving the church full time.

Speaking of the Islamic worldview, our expert on that topic, Peter Riddell, echoed Aaron on the way we've all worked together under the Kampourises.

The complementary nature of the team is quite remarkable. Each member brings specific skills and experience to the table, and those pieces then fit together like a puzzle to form a coherent whole. Being part of the *KJ* team is extremely satisfying because individual members receive respect for their own contributions, while at the same time having the opportunity to learn vast amounts of information from other members.

Ben Mitchell remembers our using elements of the colored hats system, a practice hatched originally by Edward de Bono. He worked with real hats, but we stuck to imaginary ones, using the "green hat" for brainstorming and the "black hat" for critical analysis. (de Bono's system had six—blue for management; green for creativity; white for information; red for emotion; black for discernment; and yellow for optimism—and we touched on all at one time or another, but, again, we majored on green and black.)

Speaking of colors, we soon became familiar with Camille's "green book," the one she filled with observations as she read our pieces over coffee in the mornings. Unlike the green hat of creativity, the green book was more likely to raise problems with a piece. We'd be well along to approving an article, and then she'd say, "Let me check," and we'd hold our breath as she opened the notebook.

And then there was color-coding for our articles. When the editorial team in America signed off on a piece and it was cleared with the fact-checker/proofreader, Brian Pinney labeled it BLUE and sent it to Charles for review and comments. As consulting editor, Charles sometimes addressed theology or ecclesiology, but more often, he'd explain that "Americanisms" such as baseball terms like 'first base' and 'home run' might not be understood in many countries. And he'd sometimes press us to trim things a bit "since no working pastor has the time to read long articles." Finally, the US team would review Charles's edits and comments and make adjustments as needed. The article then turned GREEN, ready for posting on the site.

Road Shows (and a Prayer on the Road)

As many as two dozen writers contributed at least one piece to the site. Once it was up and going, a number of us "hit the road" to acquaint pastors with the resource through presentations in Houston, Chicago, Belfast, London (to the Evangelical Ministry Assembly and to a group of Welsh pastors who gathered in our hotel), Washington, DC (to some Family Research Council events), and in a northwest Connecticut retreat center, where Tim Keller had assembled Redeemer Presbyterian's church planters from around the globe.

I should say a word about the role that prayer played in our work, including a great blessing God granted us on one of our trips to London. It was SOP that our editorial meetings began with prayer, and Brian Pinney regularly circulated collected requests to the team by email. But here was an instance of dire, time-sensitive petition: We'd taken taxis to a Sunday morning service at Westminster Chapel, where Martyn Lloyd-Jones was pastor for close to thirty years. As soon as we were seated, Camille discovered that she'd left her purse in the cab. (The weight of an umbrella on her arm had given her the sense that her purse was with her.) Immediately, she rushed outside, but, sure enough, the cab was gone. (It was a real crisis, for the purse contained important documents and valuables, including cash and jewelry, and their loss jeopardized the Kampouris's travel on to continental Europe to visit family.)

Two homeless men (the older of the two, reticent and much the worse for wear) turned to her, and the younger one asked if she was all right. Hearing her story, he shook his head, saying that London was a tough town and that she'd never see her purse again. Responding, she testified amiably that, if God desired, he was perfectly capable of retrieving it for her. And then she began to pray, even singing softly along with the music flowing from inside.

Standing on the front steps of the church, she was occasionally mistaken for a greeter, and greet she did as people arrived for the service.

An elder happened out and asked if he could help, and he quickly tracked down the number of the cab company. But, when called, they said it would be Monday before they could check things out. (Good luck with that.)

Then, just before the preaching began, she entered the auditorium, but not before asking the homeless men to come get her if something turned up. (Just before she went inside, I met her out front, learned of her plight, and joined her in prayer. I had an early plane to catch, and I could only stay at the church for fifteen minutes or so before catching a taxi back to the hotel to get my luggage.)

Back at the checkout desk, the clerk told me that a cabbie had driven up with a purse, and wondered if I knew anything about the owner. Well, yes! So, grabbing my stuff, I rushed outside, identified myself, and off we raced to the church.

As soon as the "street men" saw me emerge from the cab, purse in hand, the talkative one asked if it was "for the lady." Indeed, it was, so he marched into the building, right down to the front, and began walking slowly up the aisle, row by row, peering at the faithful in the pews. Disheveled, with wool cap pulled down to his eyebrows, and a scowl on his face, he looked fairly menacing. But when they spied each other, Camille waved, jumped up, and walked with him arm in arm, saying, "See! I told you. My God is able."

She rewarded her street friend and the cabbie generously for their thoughtfulness, and then she had to ask the driver how he'd found his way to the hotel. The answer was amazing: Not long after he'd left the church on that rainy morning, a man had jumped into his cab and, without much delay, directed him with authority to drive to our hotel. Handing the purse to the driver and telling him to wait, he took another cab.

Once reunited with her purse, Camille, worked through its contents, looking for anything that might have tipped off the man in the cab, but she could find nothing—no bill, no key, no brochure, no business card, nothing with the name of the hotel on it. Until, that is, she noticed in her wallet, a small claim check from the coat room of the hotel. Perhaps that was what tipped him off. But how would he know she had stayed there? She might have simply eaten there or attended a daytime meeting some time or other. Or, as Camille was beginning to suspect, he might have been an angel sent by God to bless one of his daughters, and he didn't need the claim check at all.

I'm not one to argue with that.

"Incidental" Occurrences

The major theme of this book is how God takes small beginnings—"incidental" occurrences—to generate big things. Let me mention one in closing out this chapter, one involving me. Just as the Kampourises "happened to find" Doug Baker, who "happened to mention" me, I "happened to tell" an old friend, John Kramp, about this website I'd been serving for a number of years. He checked it out and was impressed with what he saw. So, in 2016, from his position as senior vice president and group publisher (Bible) for HarperCollins, he contacted us to see if we'd be interested in talking about a linkup to publish study Bibles based on material in *Kairos Journal* and its sister website, *BibleMesh*. Indeed, we were, and four such Bibles (two each in the NIV and KJV) are out or in the works—the *Unapologetic Study Bible* (based on more than four hundred *KJ* articles) and the *Storyline Study Bible* (drawing from the articles and video texts of our seven-era *Biblical Story*). Furthermore, Zondervan chose the *BibleMesh* software platform for its academic online courses and, now, lectures from a wide range of professors (such as Gregg Allison of Southern, Scott Rae of Talbot, Gordon Fee of Regent, and Wayne Grudem of Phoenix) go out through an Emmanuel Foundation channel.

To put a finer point on it, my link with John goes back to my seminary days when I took a seminar preparing me to teach a discipleship course called *MasterLife*. It proved to be a great pastoral tool, and the little group that met in my home on Sunday nights to work through this program became treasured parishioners and friends. Then, when I heard that a sequel, *MasterBuilder,* was out (this one focusing on Christian leadership), I signed up for the training course at Ouachita Baptist University in the little town of Arkadelphia, Arkansas. It was there, in the fall of 1984, that I met John Kramp, who was assisting the author of *MasterLife*, Avery Willis. From that meeting, we crossed paths in a variety of ways though the decades leading up to John's email from HarperCollins. (I was his Sunday School teacher in Franklin, Tennessee, in the early 1990s when I worked for the SBC Executive Committee and he for the denomination's LifeWay publishing agency; and when I left Midwestern Baptist Theological Seminary on my way to church planting in Evanston, Illinois, he provided critical employment in the form of Internet research for a possible product.)

I like to imagine what we would have thought if an angel had visited us that fall in the 1980s and said something like, "This isn't going to make much sense to you, but three decades from now, you'll both be involved in producing a study Bible and in supplying an Internet platform for a major Christian publisher." My response: "Wait. Slow down. What's an Internet?"

CHAPTER 14

"Our Husbands Have to Meet." (Pierre Viret Resurfaces.)

Back around Thanksgiving 1980, when Camille was a new believer finding her way in New York, she learned that her roommate, who shared the rent, was moving to another city. Camille was headed home for Thanksgiving, and the rent was due in five days. Not knowing how she'd manage, she turned to her Christian friend, Suzanne Smart, who met her at a restaurant across the street and assured her that God was going to provide for her. Suzanne explained that God often worked at the "eleventh hour." She shouldn't worry.

Meanwhile, they noticed their waitress was wearing a cross-and-treble-clef necklace. They asked, "Are you a musician or a Christian ... or both?" "Both," she replied. They soon discovered this Christian musician also needed a roommate. Camille's prayer was answered that day, in the nick of time. Her new roommate was Jeanne.

A flute player, Jeanne subsequently met internationally renowned flautist and fairly-new Christian, James Galway (knighted Sir James in 2001) in a master class, and a courtship ensued, resulting in marriage in 1982. In the course of things, Camille sometimes found caviar and champagne in their apartment refrigerator, a sign that Galway had been in town.

Before meeting Jeanne, Galway had been something of a "wild Irish man" and twice divorced. But a change was occurring, one that gave Galway a Christian testimony and a readiness to perform in churches.

On one occasion, he appeared on *Sesame Street*, and one of Camille's characters (out of forty the cast featured on the show) was chosen to receive a flute lesson from the guest. She asked writer Norman Stiles, "How did you know I knew James Galway?" (Of course, he hadn't known this.)

Meeting Back Stage

Years later, when Camille was with her husband Mano at the Willard Hotel in Washington, DC, she ran into Jeanne, who was in town with her husband as he was performing at the Kennedy Center. Insisting that their spouses meet, Jeanne brought the Kampourises back stage after the performance, and, beginning with a twenty-five-minute conversation, a friendship was struck, such that the Galways were repeated guests of the Kampourises at their apartment in New York.

Little did Camille and Jeanne know when they met in that restaurant in 1980, they would one day share similar lifestyles, married to well-known men traveling the world. And they turned out to have a shared love for the Kampouris's New York apartment, where Galway could avoid the hotel environment and the hubbub associated with such public venues. They'd stay for as much as a month at a time. Mano came to serve for James as a source of Christian fellowship—a scarce commodity in his life.

This isn't to say that the Galways lacked for other invitations. Indeed, one of these hospitality offers provided the occasion for their first stay at the Kampouris's. Professional musicians are often invited to post-performance parties, where they're asked to perform again and to stay up well into the night in conversation with their followers. James, however, just didn't relish that lifestyle. It was exhausting to him. But, on this particular occasion, the host, a North African/Middle Eastern prince and a patron of the arts, made him an offer too hard to refuse—"Stay with me."

Not wanting to offend, Jeanne said they had an invitation from her oldest, best friend (Camille) and she hoped he would understand. He did, and they made their way to the Kampouris residence on the Upper East Side for a four-day sojourn. They got along well, and the practice has continued for decades.

I first learned of the connection when we were having lunch in the midst of an editing session at the Kampouris's home in New Jersey. As flute music was playing in the background, I spied a photo on the wall beside the table. It featured Mano with another man holding a cake (an Easter lamb cake, as it turns out), both wearing aprons and traditional white chef's hats. It seemed a long shot, but I asked if the other man in the photo was James Galway. (I'd seen him for years as a guest on the *Tonight Show* with Johnny Carson and more recently on ads for his appearances at Chicago's summer Ravinia Festival.) Well, yes, it was Galway. Turns out, they were good friends and had once joined forces to bake this masterpiece. On another occasion, during a day of editing at the Kampouris's apartment in Manhattan, Galway walked into the room and greeted us. Nice.

Humility

I think it was telling that the Kampourises didn't initiate our New Jersey conversation with, "See that picture? That's Mano with his friend, *Sir* James Galway." One of our writers, David Roach (an SBTS PhD, now serving as chief national correspondence for the SBC's *Baptist Press*) picked up on the same sort of thing.

> I'm impressed at the humility that seems to accompany the K's impressive array of business and social contacts. Occasionally they let the team know how God is working among prominent people and organizations. But they are not name droppers. They seem to want God to get the glory. For that reason, they often keep to themselves about the noteworthy

circles in which they run. One time I got a firsthand picture of their sphere of influence, however, was Mr. K's 80th birthday party. Dan Quayle's stories about playing golf with Mr. K and Peter Akinola's words about him underscored in my mind that God truly has placed him and Mrs. K in some unique circles for such a time as this.

(Speaking of celebrity encounters, in New York the Kampourises share an elevator landing with author Joan Didion, and we've crossed paths briefly a couple of times. When my Southern Seminary Colleague Hershael York named her as a favorite writer in a seminary publication article, I bought a copy of her latest book and asked if she might sign it for him, which she did, graciously.)

Keith Richards and Martha Stewart

Earlier, I mentioned Mr. K's connection with General Electric CEO Jack Welch, and he did, indeed, know some corporate heavyweights. But this savvy did not translate directly into pop culture, and we got a kick out of discovering his blind spots. One evening at dinner with a few of us, Camille told two stories revealing his relative detachment from cultural icons.

I'd asked if they'd ever flown to Europe on the Concorde, and, yes, they had, a few times. One time, they'd settled into their seats when they saw an exotically-dressed fellow making his way up the aisle. I believe she said he was wearing something like a tux, but unbuttoned from the collar down, revealing a hairy chest and some bling. He plopped down in the seat just across from them, which wasn't far away since the plane was slender. He lit a cigarette, which wasn't allowed on the Concorde, and when the flight attendant came near, Mano discretely signaled to her, pointing out the infraction. (The conversation went as follows: She said, "That's Keith Richards." Mano replied, "Yes, and he's smoking.")

With a little reluctance and caution, she told the man the rules, and they worked out a compromise—that he would move to the back row to do his smoking. So, he shuffled to the rear without hesitation or hostility.

Turns out, he was the legendary rhythm guitarist for the Rolling Stones, but for all Mr. K knew, it could have been Richard Gere, Billy Joel, or George Clinton of Parliament Funkadelic. And, of course, it didn't matter.

Camille went on to recount the story of a dinner party held to celebrate the reemergence of American Standard stock to public trading. A Goldman Sachs vice president was there, as were several couples, including Martha Stewart and her date. She arrived just a bit late, and her entry stirred excited conversation among the women, who peppered her with questions and comments throughout the first part of the evening.

At a lull in the conversation, Mano, who was seated beside her, turned to her and asked, "Do you work?" (Camille recalls that, at this point, her tomato soup [Camille's, not Martha's] almost came out her nose.) Not at all ruffled by the question, Martha described how she did some media projects—publishing and so on. It was a pleasant exchange, and the soirée continued until its happy conclusion.

The happiness did not carry over into the elevator, where Camille expressed her dismay at Mano's "gaffe." She tried to explain that Martha was a cultural institution, and he heard her out as best he could, protesting his innocence.

The next morning, while he was shaving, Camille spotted Martha on the *Today Show*. The program had moved outside to a plaza or blocked-off street, where Martha was giving tips on summer grilling. Camille rushed in to grab Mano for a look, and he obliged, only to observe after watching for a moment, "What? That's it? She's just flipping burgers?"

So yes, he knew and fraternized with remarkable, cultural elites. But this didn't mean he was an aficionado of pop culture. We found this charming.

Incidentally, at that 80th birthday party, to which David referred, the team gave the Kampourises a glass bowl, engraved by Philip Lawson Johnson, who has worked "by appointment to the Queen." He's a Christian, and he writes "Jesus Cares" on the bottom of each piece he does.

Pierre Viret

Mano and James have maintained contact through the years, and this has led to the re-publication in French of a classic by Pierre Viret, one of John Calvin's colleagues in Geneva. The book, full of biblical moral counsel, fit the Kairos template, and when the editor came to Galway for help, he turned to Mano for suggestions and assistance.

It began with a letter to Mano from Jean-Marc Berthoud, one prompted by encouragement from Galway, whom he'd met when they were students in Paris in 1960. After more than three decades, during which time they'd both become confessors of Christ, they met again when Berthoud attended a concert Galway and Jeanne gave in Lausanne. As they were catching up, Galway learned that Berthoud was now on the Committee of the Association Pierre Viret. He was in the process of republishing Viret's *Instruction chrétienne en la Loi et l'Évangile* (*Christian Instruction in the Law and the Gospel*) and seeking subsidies to make the work more affordable to the public. Berthoud, in turn, learned that Galway was friends with a Christian philanthropist who might help, and so he did, thanks to the link-up through Galway.

In the letter James passed along to Mano, Jean-Marc wrote that the work would reappear "after some 450 years of absence from the published page," and it served as "a moral practical counterpart to John Calvin's justly famous *Institutes of the Christian Religion*." Berthoud hoped:

> [I]t will be seen that Viret is no minor theologian, just good enough to sit in the wings of the heroes of the Reformation as they are depicted on the *Wall of the Reformation* in Geneva, but a theological and spiritual giant in his own right, colleague and friend, equal of John Calvin himself, betrayed before posterity by his great modesty, the simplicity and the colloquial style of his popular dialogues, and, above all, by a theology too practical for the tastes of later times much attached to a more dogmatic and abstract form of theological theorizing.

In the appendix to an article on the man, "Pierre Viret: The Apologetics and Ethics of the Reformation," Berthoud listed almost four dozen published writings of the reformer in French, a total of around twenty thousand pages. He began the piece with this hope:

> In these spiritually and doctrinally dangerous times my prayer is that God will grant his Church many courageous and lucid men who, confronted by an impious, immoral and intellectually corrupt age will not hesitate, as Cornelius Van Til did in his own time, to bravely do battle with the enemies of the faith, for the good of Christ's Church, the advance of his Kingdom and the sole glory of our Almighty and blessed God, Father, Son and Holy Spirit.

In other words, he was something of "a Kairos man."

Reading on through the paper, we discover:

- in 1531, "Guillaume Farel, that intrepid preacher of the Gospel and political agent of the newly reformed authorities of the Berne Republic, called Viret (as he would Calvin a few years later) out of the tranquility of his studies into the battlefield of the reformation of the Church and the implantation in his country of God's mighty Kingdom"

- he faced attempts on his life, first by a monk who stabbed him in the back with a sword, and second, by poisoned soup, which permanently injured his health

- he was Calvin's "most intimate friend, known under the name of *the angel of the reformation*"

- in Lausanne in 1537, he founded the first Reformed Academy (led by Theodore Beza) which, in his day, had up to a thousand students, some of whom authored the *Heidelberg Catechism*

- Beza said of his preaching, that "none has a more winsome charm when he speaks"

- Calvin said in his preface to Viret's *Christian Disputations* that he had "the talent to write aptly and with grace and thereby to speak with such joyous manner as to amuse without being in any way inept"

- he devoted hundreds of pages to "the detailed application of the Ten Commandments to every aspect of reality" and, more than Calvin, showed kinship to the Reconstructionism of a R.J. Rushdoony.

Berthoud concludes, "If his good friend, John Calvin, was the consummate dogmatician and the prince of exegetes, Pierre Viret must be considered as the finest ethicist and the most acute apologist of the [sixteenth] century."

firstflute.com

In a different vein, the Kampourises also provided funding for Galway's flute-instruction website, firstflute.com, where you find a great introduction to the man and his gifts. With his wonderful Irish accent, he recounts his beginnings with the instrument and his key influences—and you hear him play a bit of flute as well. The site also features words of commendation from the principal flautists of New York's Metropolitan Opera, Milan's La Scala, and Beijing's China National Symphony, among others.

The website bio reads, in part:

> Sir James has had the honor to perform for dignitaries from presidents to popes, emperors and queens, and shared the stage with an amazing variety of entertainers, from Pink Floyd to Jessye Norman. He also devotes much of his free time supporting many charitable organizations such as UNICEF, SOS and Youth Music (UK), amongst others. Among the many honors and awards for his musical achievements are: the Recording Academy's President's Merit Award; Classic Brits Lifetime Achievement Award; The Hollywood Bowl Hall of Fame, Artist Laureate of the Ulster Orchestra, the Lifetime Achievement Award from the National Concert Hall, Dublin, Ireland, and numerous gold and platinum CDs. He has been honored twice by Her Majesty Queen Elizabeth II, with The OBE in 1979 and again in 2001 with a knighthood for his services to music.

(I might add that, recently, I was in the book store for the Juilliard School of Music at Lincoln Center in New York. There I came across a chunky box labeled *James Galway, The Man with the Golden Flute: The Complete RCA Collection*. It contained seventy one CDs and two DVDs.)

Among the gratifying items this professional sketch doesn't mention is an encounter Galway had with a flute-playing busker in the

London Underground. The fellow was an immigrant from Eastern Europe. Galway determined that he had a "gift from God" and he sought support for him. Picking up on this commendation, the Kampourises sent a check with a letter saying that they hoped he would one day give God the glory for his musical gifting. And then they forgot about it … until, that is, years later when they received an email from this beneficiary beginning, "You may not remember me, but …" Turns out, he was in New York playing lead flute in The Metropolitan Opera's production of *Carmen*. He had tickets for them, and they were able to meet him afterwards. (And, in telling this here, I trust that we're, indeed, bringing glory to God.)

Of course, I wouldn't be talking about it at all were it not for Camille's losing her roommate in 1980, her turning to her Christian friend Suzanne Smart for encouragement and counsel, and their asking the waitress Jeanne Cinnante about her cross-and-treble-clef necklace.

CHAPTER 15

"You Remind Me of My Favorite Verse."
(Encouraging Faithful Anglicans)

As Camille recalls it, Greg Thornbury had suggested that the Kairos team take a closer look at what God was doing beyond Europe and North America, noting that there were "some pretty amazing Africans" doing Kingdom work. So, Africa was on their radar. And then came the dinner invitation to meet one of these amazing churchmen, thanks to Mark Berner, a strong Anglican and Templeton Foundation trustee, with whom Mano served on the Socrates in the City board.

At the dinner, Camille was seated next to the honored guest, Nigerian Archbishop Peter Akinola, who was leading the resistance to the gay agenda in the Anglican Worldwide Communion. (For this, Akinola was twice recognized by *Time* magazine as among the hundred most influential people in the world.) Hearing of the archbishop's efforts, Camille said, "You remind me of my favorite verse, "I searched for a man ..." To which Akinola replied, "I know it well. But in that verse, God does not find such a man. What a pity." (But it seemed, in contrast, that God was indeed finding such men today, "wall builders" who would make a better showing than the leaders condemned in ancient Jerusalem in Ezekiel 22.)

The Banquet

From this encounter grew a friendship and the inspiration to inaugurate the *Kairos Journal Award*. The first one was given to Anglican bishops from the Global South, beginning with Akinola and including Henry Orombi of Uganda, Gregory Venables of Argentina, and Datuk Yong Ping Chung of Malaysia. They were honored at a gathering of two hundred at New York's Manhattan Club, with speakers including J.I. Packer, Os Guinness, and Father Frank Pavone of Priests for Life, who led the invocation.

Mr. Kampouris gave each recipient a monetary award for personal ministry and an engraved Tiffany silver tray. Each of the wives received flowers, presented by Sherry Phillips, Pastor Bob's wife.

Since this was the first gathering of so many luminaries who'd just heard of the *Journal*, we put together the aforementioned introductory video, which traced the pattern of Christian advocacy, from opposition to Rome's gladiatorial spectacles, to repudiation of Spartan infanticide, to the push for child labor laws in England. The banquet program featured a two-page spread of "kairos" verses, including 1 Chronicles 12:32 (regarding the men of Issachar who "understood the times"), Ecclesiastes 3:7 ("a time to be silent and a time to speak"), and Romans 5:6 ("at the right time Christ died for the ungodly").

Edge

As we put the journal together and framed that evening's program, I was reminded of a distinction sketched at a magazine publication workshop I attended in New York in the early 1990s, one held by *Folio* (the magazine about magazines). I was about the task of launching a new denominational paper (*SBC LIFE*), and I was getting up to speed on everything from the contrasting virtues of newsprint and coated paper to the periodical market, which was favoring niche publications over general interest offerings. Not long into the curriculum, one speaker said we needed to decide straight off whether we were going to put out something with edge, or without. Those "without" were overwhelmingly inoffensive to the average citizen—something along the lines of a Martha Stewart decorating periodical, *Reader's Digest, Saturday Evening Post,* or an issue of *Ideals Christmas* magazine. On the other hand, those with edge advanced strong, "divisive" opinions, as in such politically freighted magazines as *The Nation* and *National Review.* (Of course, as editor, I made room for "edgy" material since the Bible we used as our plumb line was quite edgy in its own right.)

The notion of 'edge' complemented another analogy that came to my mind while composing a sermon some years ago. I'd recently seen an ad for a Nerf brand baseball and bat, both covered generously with foam rubber. They were so soft and light that you could almost play baseball in your living room with figurines displayed about, and nothing would get broken. On the other hand, real baseball—hardball—is serious business, and things can, indeed, get broken. So, the question arises whether one is leading or attending a "Nerf-church," where it's all a matter of positive thinking and warm, fuzzy feelings. Or does the church play some hardball, where the no-nonsense Word of God is in play?

Of course, there is much in Scripture that offers comfort and encouragement. Indeed, the gospel is full of grace, and the Holy Spirit as well as the fellowship of saints administers the "oil of gladness" throughout our lives. However, to exclude the bad news is to undermine the good news, rob the church of its prophetic power, and cheat the world out of its moral counsel.

Here are some selections from the often-edgy remarks of both presenters and honorees that evening.

Os Guinness

Let's begin with Os Guinness, who let it be known right off that we were there to play hardball.

Soren Kierkegaard called them "kissing Judases," followers of Jesus who betray him with an interpretation. Following Friedrich Schleiermacher's famous plea that Christians reach out to the "cultured despisers of the gospel," we are seeing a troubling growth of those who bend every nerve to reach the cultured despisers of the gospel, and then join them, and become like them ... But beyond any doubt, one of the worst and most extreme capitulations to the spirit of the age are the leaders of the American Episcopal Church and their abject surrender to the sexual mores of the modern world. At one level the result is an *Alice in Wonderland* church in which Christian leaders now openly deny what all Christians have believed and many have died to defend. Christian leaders who now celebrate what Christian leaders once castigated ... Christian leaders who deny the faith but stay on shamelessly as leaders of the faith they deny. But at a deeper level, these treacherous leaders are a shame and a disgrace to their master, and their fellow believers, and I believe that like Judas, they are pursuing a suicidal path.

Henry Orombi

Next came Archbishop Henry Luke Orombi, who, after quoting Revelation 2:10 ("Be faithful even to the point of death, and I will give you the crown of life.") spoke of the church of Uganda, saying it had "passed through several fires." The first was the "fire of martyrdom" in the late 1880s, when King Mwanga executed over forty young Christian men by beheading and by fire because they would not give in to his sexual advances. (We have a *Kairos Journal* article on their martyrdom, an event celebrated in Uganda each June 3.) "You think sexual perversion began two, three, ten years ago. We in Uganda, by 1886, were resisting it," Orombi said. The second fire was the "fire of the 1935 East African revival," which started in Rwanda and spilled over into Uganda, Kenya, and Tanzania. Orombi said the revival "brought conviction, repentance, and restitution to those who had been caught up in the blaze." Finally, there was the "fire of persecution (1971-1979), when the Muslim dictator Idi Amin strove to make Uganda an Islamic country." It meant the martyrdom of Orombi's forerunner, Archbishop Junani Luwum, who had protested Amin's reign of terror. Luwum had joined the "cloud of witnesses" whose example inspires the Ugandan church. (His wife had urged him to flee persecution, but he responded, "To whom will I leave the ship?")

(As a footnote, Camille recounts an exchange between Princeton Professor Robert George and Archbishop Orombi. George asked him, "Why are you doing this?" Orombi replied, "I won't lead my flock to hell.")

Datuk Yong Ping Chung

Next rose Archbishop Datuk Yong Ping Chung from the province of the Anglican Church of Southeast Asia, with nine nations and over 450 million people (in Malaysia, Singapore, Brunei, Indonesia, Vietnam, Cambodia, Thailand, Laos, and Nepal). His parish had the largest Muslim population on earth, but had strong representation from Buddhism, Taoism, Confucianism, Hinduism, animism, ancestral worship, and mysticism. Christianity was something of a latecomer to the region, and believers amounted to only a small minority—less than 8 percent in Malaysia, for instance. Many had sought in vain to escape the bondage of human sin, but leaving the faith of their ethnic group, family, culture, and tradition had exacted a high cost for "traitors." In this context, he said, "Choosing to follow Jesus is not something to be taken lightly. To be a Christian demands commitment and sacrifices. It is a matter of life or death. Yes, it is a matter of eternal life or eternal death."

As difficult as the external challenges might be, he continued,

> [T]oday we have a much greater obstacle and a much greater stumbling block to overcome. That is, the problem from within our own communions. The

very churches who brought us the gospel so many years ago are now telling us that none of this matters at all. "After all," they say, "Jesus is not the only way, not the only truth, and not the only life. There are many ways to God." ... Sin is now out of fashion. Only those fundamentalists, like many of you here, will insist on that. Now there is no need for repentance, for, after all, "God so loved the world." ... There is no such thing as the power of God to change lives. After all, God accepts you as you are. Whatever you do, even marrying someone of your own sex, is fine as long as it makes you happy, brings you human dignity, and fulfills so-called justice. They have forgotten, brothers and sisters, that we can have no true peace, no true happiness, no true dignity, and no true justice without Jesus Christ.

He went on to say that the behavior of those who have drifted makes evangelism very difficult:

Many people in our land are now very confused ... We have to stand up ... and confront the churches that brought us the gospel and say to them. "No, no. What you are trying to advocate now is not the same as the gospel you brought us long ago. The gospel you brought us long ago set us free from the bondage of sin and the pains of our land, but what you are telling us now brings only confusions and brings us back into the bondage of the darkness of sins."

J.I. Packer

Another of the introducers, J.I Packer, offered this perspective:

I accept this privilege with a heavy heart. It isn't all joy, for I too am an Anglican, and I too, like the brothers who will be speaking to you in a moment, as well as the two who have spoken already, I am involved in the agony of world Anglicanism at this present time. I never dreamed that when my ministry started over half a century ago that I should find myself in the position where I am today with the Anglican communion coming apart all around me ...

I speak to you as one of those who, without realizing what we were doing, threw a stone into the Anglican pond, which sent ripples throughout the whole communion. I was one of the eighty folks representing ten parishes in the diocese of New Westminster, Canada, who declared ourselves out of communion with our bishop and our synod when the synod asked the bishop to institute the blessing of same-sex unions. And when the bishop said he would do that, we declared ourselves immediately to be out of communion with them because they had denied the gospel. And we walked out of the synod to show that we meant it. That was the beginning of the association called the Anglican Communion in New Westminster, which continues in the diocese seeking to be a voice that will bring the diocese to Christian sanity and repentance ...

This is a denial of the authority of the Bible because it is a denial of the gospel of Jesus Christ which is the true interpretation of Scripture. The Bible identifies this kind of behavior as sin, and the gospel declares that the way of salvation is faith in Christ with repentance from sin. And there is no way of salvation without repentance from sin. And Paul says that terribly clearly in 1 Corinthians 6:9 ...

The gentlemen in whom I am in the process of introducing are heroes as it seems to me, because they see the issues clearly, and, at the risk of being blackballed by the, may I say, the Mister Moneybags of the Anglican Communion, that is the Episcopal Church of the States, at the risk of suffering ostracism from that quarter, they have taken a stand …

Here's a definition of leadership I picked up from somewhere: "Leaders are visionaries with a poorly-developed sense of fear and no concept of the odds against them." Friends, it is men of that caliber whose leadership we are celebrating tonight.

Gregory Venables

Then, the third of the honorees, Gregory Venables, Primate of the Southern Cone, supplied his observations.

Hebrews chapter two, verse one says, "We must pay greater attention to what we've heard, so as not to drift away." We must pay greater attention, not to what we think, or to what we feel, or to what we've experienced, but to what we have heard, what God has said … lest we drift away. What has happened, my dear friends, my dear brothers and sisters: The Church has failed to pay attention to what we've heard, and the church has drifted away.

He then laid much of the blame at the feet of the biblically orthodox, who've taken counsel of their fears, withdrawn into themselves, and lost the passion for missions, which once motivated the faithful. This was the impetus for his leaving England for Argentina in 1977. He closed saying, "We in the Global South are committed to the re-evangelization of the United States and Canada and Great Britain, but we want to do it with you."

Peter Akinola

Working from the example of the church in Sardis, Archbishop Akinola added this warning:

> The Church today—America, Nigeria, England, everywhere—has the semblance of being alive, but, on closer examination, you'll find that most of the church today is fast asleep. And unless we wake up, as God gives chance ... that sleep remains as sleep to death.

Aake Green

The next day, the *KJ* team met back at the hotel, where we spent time with a special guest, Aake Green, a Pentecostal pastor in his sixties from a little Swedish island where the cows outnumbered the people. When, the year before, he'd heard about a "gay pride" event in Stockholm, he set himself to compose a sermon on homosexuality, starting his study in the fall, and looking toward delivery in the spring to coincide with the parade.

He'd asked himself, "What can I do? What can I hope to accomplish? My church is so small and my members are old." But he pressed ahead, convinced that God had told him to preach on the subject.

Once he'd written the sermon, he contacted the local radio station to announce his forthcoming message, thinking it might draw seekers-of-biblical-wisdom to hear it. This was, of course, naïve, or quite courageous. The backlash was fierce, and he was charged with a form of "hate speech," resulting in a fine.

He appealed the judgment, and the case went all the way to the Supreme Court of Sweden, where he was asked what exactly he'd said. He was able, in essence, to re-preach the sermon, this time to a nation listening in on the radio. The court exonerated him, which was nice, but another nation did one better. While the case was pending, Poland invited him to address its Parliament, thus honoring him for his stand.

None of this was in Aake's plan. He was a humble man who simply wanted to preach a biblical sermon on an issue of the day. He's wasn't an activist, but God drafted him for a very public performance for the cause of truth and decency. (We tell the story in more detail on our website.)

Manhattan Declaration

In the years that followed the awards banquet, the gay agenda continued to gain ground in the West, and *Kairos Journal* gave it extensive attention, with scores of articles devoted to the topic, including eleven pertinent Bible studies.

This social malady was the impetus for a gathering—something of a strategic briefing and strength rally—the Kampourises funded at the Manhattan Club, one that drew on the work of the National Organization for Marriage and the successful efforts of the Californians who'd advanced Proposition 8, which amended the state's constitution to describe marriage as only valid when between one man and one woman. (That amendment was overturned by the state's Supreme Court in the following year). The meeting was planned for the afternoon and evening, but then a call came from Chuck Colson, who asked if he might piggyback a session devoted to a document in the works, one to be called the "Manhattan Declaration." The Kampourises agreed.

Some thought the document was a little long, and the Ks and Colson asked me to attempt a condensed version. I came up with a two-page adaptation, but they decided that the full text was worth keeping. There was too much good stuff in the original.

The Manhattan Declaration meeting came in the morning and was a smaller affair, with a remarkable invitation list crafted largely by Colson. The presentations were stirring and the audience was receptive. Almost all went on to sign the Declaration, built around three causes: 1) the sanctity of life; 2) the sanctity of marriage; and 3) religious liberty. These three matters were front and center in our thinking at *Kairos Journal*, but there was an added element in the discussion which struck me particularly that day. Not only were we saying we believed in these things, but that we were also ready to go to jail for them. We were drawing a line, saying, in effect, to the opposing forces, "Are you prepared for the challenge of thousands of pastors appearing at the court house to turn themselves in for disobeying your edicts forbidding them to speak the deep and biblical truths you find offensive? Are your jails big enough to handle all the Christians who refuse to knuckle down to your perverse speech codes and affronts to the First Amendment?" It was exhilarating.

This isn't to say there were no tensions in the effort. The theological dynamic was electric. Since the Declaration itself cited Christian stands throughout history, and the examples were both Catholic and Protestant, some were convinced that we were ignoring doctrinal differences and harsh judgments. A number of Reformed pastors withheld support because it seemed to say the Reformation was a triviality. A number of Catholics were having to hold their tongues when Southern Seminary President Al Mohler was tapped to deliver the keynote address. After all, in some of his writing, he had said some pretty tough things about Rome. (When the dust settled, the Manhattan Declaration garnered more than five hundred thousand signatories through its website.)

Speaking of "co-belligerents," I enjoyed sitting at the luncheon table with Dr. Mohler and Archbishop (now Cardinal) Dolan of New York. The conversation was congenial, as were the remarks of a priest with whom I shared an elevator after the evening's banquet. He somewhat grudgingly observed that Mohler had really rung the bell in his speech. (Incidentally, in that address, Mohler, who, as a Southern

Baptist minister/seminary employee, doesn't drink alcoholic beverages, thanked Cardinal Dolan for helping him to navigate among the various glasses at his luncheon place setting earlier in the day.)

Still, there were limits to our ecumenism. Protestants and Catholics alike agreed that Mormons lay outside the pale of orthodoxy, so they were not invited to sign. But some Mormons were present in the afternoon meeting and were honored for their efforts in California. Incidentally, Proposition 8's passage surprised some party leaders since normally-Democrat black voters broke ranks and voted with Republicans on this measure.

By that time, the California victory was far from lonely, for similar measures had passed in thirty states. Only the Massachusetts Supreme Court and the New York legislature had championed gay marriage, despite the apparent groundswell of public indignation at the cause. Now, we were on the brink of a big test, the referendum in Maine, not known for its Bible Belt convictions, and Maggie Gallagher, head of National Organization for Marriage, briefed us on the "ground war." (To the surprise of many of us, Maine soon joined California, putting the new total at thirty-one.)

About a year later, the Kampourises hosted a follow-up meeting, again at the Manhattan Club. And again, it was a Catholic and Protestant affair. Cardinal Dolan and Robert George, a professor from Princeton University, represented the former. Rick Warren, a Southern Baptist, was one of the latter.

Mark Regnerus

Particularly telling was a presentation by Mark Regnerus, a professor at the University of Texas who'd studied the impact of lesbian parentage on children (women being the overwhelming majority of homosexual couples raising children). He debunked an earlier study from San Francisco, which had served as inspiration and warrant for the movie, *The Kids Are All Right*.

With funding from the Witherspoon Foundation, he'd surveyed more than a thousand lesbian households, checking for incidences of school failure, contemplation of suicide, substance abuse, etc., comparing those numbers with those found in other homes without homosexual parents (for example, with a widowed or divorced parent raising kids alone). The statistics were powerful, revealing a ratio of 4:1 in certain pathologies.

For this, Regnerus had paid a price. Colleagues at his Texas university said his work had been shabby, and they challenged his fitness for promotion and tenure. A committee was convened, and it concluded that his standards were as high as those of his critics, so he was cleared. (Of course, if his findings had been pro-gay, there would have been no dustup at all.)

In the end, the Supreme Court (following the same pattern of judicial arrogance they displayed regarding abortion in *Roe v. Wade*) dismissed the convictions and laws of the majority, enshrined in state laws, and swept aside all barriers to gay marriage in their decision in *Obergefell v. Hodges*.

GAFCON

Having honored Akinola and his fellow conservative bishops, the Kampourises were sympathetic —indeed, enthusiastic—toward the emergence of the Global Anglican Future Conference (GAFCON), with connections to conservative Anglican congregations in America who left the Episcopal Church in the USA (ECUSA) to align with Global South bishops, and with the budding American bodies— the Convocation of Anglicans in North America (CANA) and the Anglican Church in North America (ACNA).

The first gathering, a crisis meeting in Jerusalem, took place in June 2008. As Charles Marnham recalls, it was a "hairy, tricky" undertaking, but the result was gratifying. It reminded him of one of the early church councils, marked by accord and unity.

Mano and Camille were encouraged that Charles was on board. Of course, he was familiar with the denominational situation in England, and he'd been stirred by the Kairos event in New York, but his fellowship with like-minded Anglicans in the developing world began in Africa in the late 1990s. He spoke of this at a writers camp dinner in DC in 2002.

> A few years ago, I was put in touch with a wonderful Christian leader—Donald Mtetemela—Anglican Bishop of Ruaha in Central Tanzania, and now also the Archbishop of Tanzania. We set up a link between St. Michael's in London and his Diocese, and as I expected, we have learned so much.

> Tanzania has been ravaged by drought, famine and the scourge of AIDS. The Christians have pitifully few resources both in terms of finance and trained personnel. They also face a real threat from aggressive and militant Islam. Pastors have to grow their own food, and there are no pensions when they retire.

> The archbishop has given his diocese a Millennium Challenge—ten new churches with ten new pastors and ten new evangelists. They are well on the way to achieving that. At the last Lambeth Conference for bishops from the worldwide Anglican Communion, he worked fearlessly and successfully to maintain the biblical teaching on homosexuality, despite sustained pressure from some Western bishops. He has gone against his culture in refusing to employ members of his own or extended family to avoid any accusations of nepotism or corruption …

> There is a cost to all this—he suffers from regular bouts of malaria. He has to travel long arduous

journeys on Tanzania's dangerous roads, and he is
frequently away from home. But both in preaching
the gospel and in speaking out in the public square,
he has proved himself indeed to be God's watchman.

This was the sort of leader attracted to GAFCON, and the
Kampourises were pleased to help with funding the meeting.

Michael Ovey

Subsequently, they attended the October 2013 meeting in Nairobi,
whose host-city selection was a great encouragement to the church
there, and to Africa in general. Though Nigeria has more Anglicans,
Kenya's fellowship is also strong, and the Kenyans proved to be ad-
mirable hosts to the more than 1,300 delegates from thirty-eight
nations. Marnham remembers particularly, the "terrific lectures"
offered the attendees, especially one by Michael Ovey, late principal
of Oak Hill College in London, who died all too young in January
2017. Ovey's lecture was titled, "The Grace of God OR the World of
the West?"[25]

Ovey began by recalling a chapel address he heard in 1990 from an
East African priest visiting England. He was struck especially hard
by the question, "Which gospel do you westerners want us to believe?
The one you came with or the one you preach now?" Ovey went on to
say that the issue was the West's embrace of what Dietrich Bonhoeffer
called "cheap grace" in *The Cost of Discipleship*:

> Cheap grace is the grace we bestow on ourselves.
> Cheap grace is the preaching of forgiveness without
> requiring repentance, baptism without church dis-
> cipline, communion without confession … Cheap
> grace is grace without discipleship, grace without
> the cross, grace without Jesus Christ, living and
> incarnate.

Ovey went on to note that the Western church has done its share of repenting, such as for racism and the murder of indigenous peoples. We Christians and the world at large agree that we needed to confess those wrongs and change our ways—"Where we do repent, we repent of the things that the world finds offensive." But "the acid test of whether our repentance is really towards God is when God and the world disagree." And sexual sins are a case in point, which "the Western churches are increasingly disinclined to condemn."

Ovey also quoted from an eighteenth-century Anglican homily to declare,

> "For of ourselves we be crab trees, that can bring forth no apples. We be of ourselves of such earth, as can bring forth but weeds, nettles, brambles, briers, cockle, and darnel." Yet we press on in vanity, with a sense of entitlement, a penchant for narcissism, and a susceptibility to exorbitant rights claims, yet without foundation and a sense of correlative duties.

And he concluded by saying,

> The world's needs are many, we all know that, but this is its greatest need, that its sins be forgiven. And that is why it is absolutely imperative that we at GAFCON preach not cheap grace, but costly grace to the world, not because we hate the world but because we love it, as our Savior did.

Guarantor

At the Nairobi meeting, Mano took part in a breakout session, along with Brian O'Donoghue, the brother of one of the *Kairos Journal* writers, Mark O'Donoghue. The discussion moved to how they might extend the organization beyond the archbishops to the people in the pews and how a legal structure might be framed for purposes of strength and continuity. From this emerged the role of guarantor, and Mano was enlisted to serve as one. It's a labor of love, and both he and Camille have attended some of the meetings, including one in Ireland in late 2017.

Speaking of 2017 and GAFCON's growing strength, Archbishop Nicholas Okoh, Archbishop Akinola's successor in 2010, now chairs the primate's council. He was present at Wheaton College in June 2017 when Foley Beach, archbishop of the Anglican Church in North America, commissioned Andrew Lines as missionary bishop for Scotland and Europe under GAFCON. Of the 1,400 delegates to the meeting, fifty were bishops and archbishops, who laid hands on Lines in the ceremony.

A postscript: Though GAFCON rose out of opposition to such leadership as was offered by the openly-homosexual American Bishop Gene Robinson, the organization has shifted attention to the positive biblical causes of missions and evangelism.

CHAPTER 16

"I Want You to Meet Herb." (A Fruitful Jewish Friendship)

Vice-President Dan Quayle was on Mano's American Standard board and that of the Hudson Institute, whose president, Herb London, once led the Great Books program at New York University and who once garnered the most votes ever for a third-party candidate for governor of New York. Founded at Croton-on-Hudson in 1961, the Institute moved to Indiana in 1984, where it operated until 2004, when it moved to Washington. Quayle, a conservative Hoosier, had connected naturally with Hudson, and now he wanted to bring Mano on board—indeed, on the board. Mano agreed, and the relationship has proven quite fruitful. Some of this I cover in the next chapter. But here, I'll focus on two items, the Vienna Conference and our trip to Israel with Friends of the Israeli Defense Forces. I'll also talk a bit about our *Kairos Journal* Award for Daniel Scot.

Vienna Conference

In 2007, Mano, Herb London, and John O'Sullivan, former editor of *National Review*, teamed up to host a conference at Schloss Neuwaldegg, a retreat center on the heights above Vienna, not far from the site where, in 1683, Jan Sobieski, the "Hammer of Christendom," turned back Muslim forces. This prevented the Islamization of Europe from the east. (Sobieski was not unlike Charles Martel, who, in AD 732, defeated a Muslim army not far from Paris, the city toward which they'd marched from their base in

Iberia, which they'd already conquered.) The conference focused on the simultaneous expansion of Islam in Europe and the decline, even collapse, of the European church. (Herb and John characterized the Kairos team as the "Christian think tank" for the event.)

Prudentially, the meeting was closed and confidential, for the topic was quite inflammatory. Salman Rushdie had been under an Iranian *fatwa* (in this case, an execution order) since 1988 for his novel playing off what have been called the "satanic verses" in the Koran. Theo Van Gogh had been stabbed to death in 2004 in the Netherlands for his documentary, *Submission*, depicting the sorry plight of Muslim women—a film produced with the assistance of Ayaan Hirsi Ali. In 2005, the Danish newspaper *Jyllands-Posten* had suffered enormous backlash for publishing a dozen irreverent Muhammad cartoons. These deplorable events helped underscore the need for such a conference.

The participants included members of several European parliaments, secular journalists, church leaders, editors, and think tank members, many of them not Christian and some not observant in any faith. The conference thesis was that Europe could only have developed— and could only be sustained—with a Judeo-Christian base; thus, as foundations for society, neither secularism nor Islam were sufficient for the task. Indeed, they were wobbly and brittle.

Not surprisingly, there was pushback in the house, especially when four of us from the *Kairos Journal* team—Peter Riddell, Ben Mitchell, Greg Thornbury, and I—read our papers and fielded questions as a panel in the Sunday morning session. We quoted Roger Scruton to say of Western Civilization, "Its basic fund of stories, its moral precepts, and its religious imagery come from the Hebrew Bible and the Greek New Testament." And we added a word from crusading atheist Christopher Hitchens: "You are not educated if you don't know the Bible. You can't read Shakespeare or Milton without it …"

We went on to trace the Judeo-Christian roots of constitutionalism (with its limited powers of government); the notion of universal human rights (with defense of the dignity and sanctity of all); equal esteem for both genders and all races; provision for creative and economic freedom; the repudiation of infanticide and gladiatorial brutality; the concept of vocation; the right to property; the rise of science and medicine; the establishment of hospitals and other humanitarian institutions (It's hard to find a Friedrich Nietzsche Orphanage or a Special Olympics team named for Jean-Jacques Rousseau or Bertrand Russell); freedom of conscience and expression; just war standards; and the flourishing of the arts.

Our presentations were subsequently folded into a booklet, *Legatees of a Great Inheritance: How the Judeo-Christian Tradition Has Shaped the West* (now available online to registrants at *kairosjournal.org*). We all pitched in on every page of the booklet, but I took special pleasure in addressing the arts on a couple of pages. While recognizing such striking Muslim achievements as the Taj Mahal (built by the Mughals in India) and the Alhambra palace (built by the Moors in Spain), Islam cannot begin to match the great variety of offerings across the range of Western/Judeo-Christian art forms: painting (Giotto, Botticelli, Brueghel, Durer); sculpture (Bernini and Rodin); and architecture (with Romanesque, Baroque, Neo-Classical, Italiante, Spanish mission, Colonial, Federal, Art Deco, Bauhaus, Post-Modern options, and such structures as Versailles, the residential Fallingwater in rural Pennsylvania, and the "Gherkin" in London).

The sampler continues with music (with the specifically Christian forms alone extending to oratorio, cantata, hymn, gospel song, requiem mass, Negro spiritual, and Gregorian chant); fiction (with the novel, an invention and mainstay of Western Civilization, from *Don Quixote* to *Pride and Prejudice* to *The Old Man and the Sea*); theater (with such playwrights as Shakespeare, Ibsen, and Chekov, and such venues as the Globe in London, the Abbey in Dublin, and the Guthrie in Minneapolis); film (with such prominent studios as MGM in America, Shepperton in England, Cinecittà in Italy, and Pathé in France); and comedy (with its array of satirists, comedians, cartoonists, parodists, caricaturists, clowns, and jesters, many of them from the Jewish line of our Judeo-Christian heritage, with such surnames as Brooks, Caesar, Berle, Seinfeld, Allen, Sellers, Wilder, Crystal, Lewis, Rickles, Benny, Stiller, Reiner, Burns, Rivers, and Marx).

Of course, much that comes through the arts is sub-Christian or even anti-Christian, but that is much to the point—that, over the long haul, Judeo-Christian culture has been marked by freedom, something that cannot be said for Islamic culture.

There was some grumbling by those who felt we had puffed up the religious aspect, attendees who were keen to give overarching credit to the Enlightenment. But we stuck with our position, and one reluctant journalist conceded that, after being exposed to the rival perspectives (he called them, respectively, "Vienna" and "Talladega"—the latter picking up on the Southern Baptist connections of Mitchell, Thornbury, and Coppenger), he found Talladega more compelling.

FIDF

For several years, Herb London had been a member of the FIDF, the Friends of the Israeli Defense Forces, which had raised more than $50 million to support Israeli troops and their families. The money has gone to a wide variety of causes, including construction of recreation centers and synagogues for soldiers serving in the Negev; hardship flights for foreign nationals serving in the Israeli army; basic household appliances for the families of Ethiopian Jewish immigrants, so the troops wouldn't feel pressured to go AWOL to provide for their parents, spouses, and children; and university scholarships for those who'd completed their active duty assignments.

Of course, FIDF membership is overwhelmingly Jewish, but there are Gentile supporters as well, and Herb sought to extend these ranks by inviting some non-Jewish opinion shapers and philanthropists on a familiarization tour of Israel in 2011, with extraordinary access to the military leadership and service members in the field. He included the Kampourises, and they asked that I might accompany them as a writer, given my military background. So, off we went, a mixture of Jews and Gentiles, including a minor-league baseball team owner, a black conservative radio host, an heir to a prominent jewelry company, a political columnist, and an award-winning stage and screen actor (Tony Lo Bianco, who played "Sal" in *The French Connection*, and whom Sharon and I later saw on stage as New York Mayor Fiorella La Guardia in *The Little Flower*).

We enjoyed astonishing exposure to prominent personalities—current and former generals and government ministers, with nicknames (according to Israeli practice) like "Bogie," "Chayni," and, yes, "Bibi." One official had played a key role in the 1976 Entebbe raid; another had flown a jet in the 1981 raid to knock out the Iraqi nuclear reactor at Osirak.

As for sites, we had tours of and briefings at the electronic listening post atop Mount Hermon, Iron Dome radar and launch positions near Rehoboth, and a drone base on the Mediterranean coast, about half way between Tel Aviv and the old Philistine town of Ashdod. We met with members of the Maglan special forces unit in the North and the Oketz canine unit in the South and were present at the commissioning of paratroopers at the Western Wall in an evening ceremony.

As fascinating as military topics and equipment were to this old soldier (commissioned through ROTC in 1970 and retired in 1998), the moral and spiritual aspects of the trip were striking—much of it grist for my seminary course in the ethics of peace and war. The booklet that came from it—*Israel and Legitimacy: Modern Achievement vs. Islamic Prejudice*—has enjoyed wide circulation. While our team's Australian scholar, Peter Riddell, was not along on the trip, he wrote an excellent first half, the part about Islamic prejudice, and I focused on Israel's achievements. (This booklet is also available to registered users at *kairosjournal.org*.) On a personal level, I was particularly taken by:

- The diversity of opinion among three employees of the center-left paper, *Ha'aretz*, who spent a morning with us in our Tel Aviv hotel. (As one of several who supplied religion and ethics clips to *Kairos Journal's* daily news feature, with my assignment being the online press of the world, I already knew the Israeli news landscape was full of contentious voices, from the *Jerusalem Post* to *Debka File*. But I was a little surprised to see our visitors from the same paper sparring amongst each other. It encouraged me to see journalists committed to the give and take which is inimical to tyranny, convinced the emergence and preservation of truth depends upon the free market of ideas and the recognition that fallen man needs checks and balances to keep him honest.)

- The emphasis on "Purity of Arms" (the just war principle of regard for non-combatants) taught at the military center on Ammunition Hill in Jerusalem (site of a ferocious battle during the Six-Day War in 1967).

- The video they showed us at Palmachim featuring drone footage showing their restraint in taking out a man who had launched missiles from beside a UN school in Gaza into a civilian sector in Israel. (The drone operators waited till he was well-clear of the school and people in the street.)

- The comment at the "canine corps" base that they'd stopped using the dogs to search the inside of buses out of respect for the sensitivities of Muslims, who consider dogs vile.

- The example of the Hula Valley north of the Sea of Galilee. (For centuries, it had been a fever swamp under Muslim Ottoman rule, but Israel soon turned it into a national "breadbasket," while preserving some wetlands so important to migratory birds.)

- The armored bus we took from Jerusalem to the heights above Nablus (the biblical Shechem), now under the control of the Palestinian authority. (The reason we needed this special protection was the history of sniper fire along this highway, even directed at Israeli school buses.)

- Prime Minister Benjamin Netanyahu's observation they were dealing with an enemy more like the Japanese of World War II than the Russians of the Cold War. (The essential difference was the Russians didn't want to die, and so they would respond to threats of force; on the other hand, the Japanese and Islamists were quite ready to die and even gloried it in, as with *kamikaze* pilots and bomb-vest terrorists.)

- The moment at which new paratroopers were given a copy of the *Tanakh* (Old Testament) at their induction in a nighttime ceremony at the Wailing/Western Wall. (Of course, there is much secularism in Israel, but this gesture of respect for their spiritual heritage was significant, a symbol of grounding in and dependence upon the counsel and favor of God.)

I'd first visited Israel in 1966, the summer before the Six-Day War stopped Syrian shelling from atop the Golan Heights, a rain of fire forcing farmers in the Jezreel Valley to flee with their families into bunkers. Israeli planes also neutralized the Egyptian Air Force, which was standing ready to support Egyptian President Abdel Nasser's effort to close Israel's sea lane off the southeast tip of Sinai. And Israeli infantry reclaimed the Mount of Olives and areas on the West Bank seized in the attack by five Arab nations in the days after Israel's birth.

Again, a word on the booklet. Peter discussed the grounding and rise of anti-Semitism in the Qur'an, the Hadith (traditions regarding the sayings and deeds of Muhammad), and the commentaries—a perspective reflected in the scathing Hamas Covenant, which calls for ongoing struggle against the Jews and the subjugation of Israel.

And it also debunked the claim the Old Testament has been altered to shortchange Muhammad.

In the second part, I surveyed the features of Israel not manifest in her circling and often hostile neighbors—democracy; a free press; stewardship of resources (including "making the desert bloom" and "draining the swamps"); globally beneficial ingenuity (including medical research); high status for women; and refuge for Jews from around the world. As England's chief rabbi Jonathan Sacks observed, "Today there are eighty-two Christian nations and fifty-six Muslim ones, but only one Jewish one: in a country smaller than the Kruger National Park [in South Africa], one quarter of one percent of the land mass of the Arab world." And, as we argue in the booklet, this small country has distinguished itself so dramatically that it stands as a testimony to the cultural failings of its enemies.

I remember the strong impression I had in 1966 when passing from Jordanian-controlled territory into Israel (through the Mandelbaum Gate in Jerusalem). I felt as though I was moving from Bible Lands into Southern California—into Western Civilization. And so it was, for Israel is the product of the Judeo-Christian culture, and that makes all the difference. The 2011 trip was graphic demonstration of the point we made at the 2007 conference in Vienna. You couldn't fashion Europe and the West out of just any old religious culture.

Daniel Scot

The 2007 Vienna conference came on the heels of a special event in New York in January, bestowal of a *Kairos Journal* Award on Daniel Scot, a Pakistani immigrant to Australia, forced to flee because of his Christian witness in his homeland. Scot was a university professor, who had to pass an exam on the Koran before appointment, a test he mastered. He did well as a professor too, and that was the problem. If he'd been invisible, Islamists might have left him alone. But, as a Muslim colleague warned him, there was a move to neutralize his Christian influence, and he needed to leave before he got hurt.

He'd been summoned to appear before a counsel of five senior professors who wanted to investigate him for sharing the gospel. They began with flattering him for his great work in mathematics, but they said his life was in danger now and the only way they could help him was if he became Muslim. He decided to speak to them of salvation. He asked them who would save their souls. The response, "Muhammad." And then he quoted chapter (surah) and verse where Muhammad said he didn't know what would happen to even himself in the afterlife. So, if he didn't know where he was going—and he might be in hell—how could he save us?

Not surprisingly, continued residence and work in Pakistan became untenable. So, he found his way to Melbourne, where he gained another opportunity to teach math at the University of Queensland.

Then, 9/11 and the Bali bombings happened, the latter killing eighty-eight Australians in 2002. A local church asked Scot to give a talk, explaining what was happening, and he did so from experience and with both clarity and love. Another church asked him to do the same, and word got around, not only among Christians, but also among Muslims, some of whom came to a service primed to be offended.

Though Scot was the model of Christian civility, and though he longed for the conversion of Muslims, he was also a truth teller, and this stirred the guests to bring a suit against him on the charge of "vilification of religion," under the Racial and Religious Tolerance Act of 2001. Finding a sympathetic Judge Michael Higgins in the Victorian Civil and Administrative Tribunal, they gained a decision directing Scot and a pastor to take out $75,000 in ads in local papers apologizing to Muslims. But they refused and appealed, at great expense, to the Supreme Court of Victoria. They won. The case was remanded to the trial court with the stipulation Higgins not be involved. And they forced the Muslim plaintiffs to share the considerable court costs. The whole expensive process took longer than five years—and this in a "liberal" Western democracy.

Hearing of the courage and plight of this brother before he was exonerated, the Kampourises chose him for the second *Kairos Journal* Award, and I had the privilege of calling to tell him. Of course, he'd never heard of us, and he was nonplussed to get the news. It was an emotional exchange as I tried to explain who we were and what this was, but, as the reality dawned on him, he offered thanks and said that he and his wife, Mariat, had just been talking about whether and how they would ever dig out of their financial hole.

Though we didn't have the solution to all his problems, the offer was helpful—a monetary award and transportation for him and his wife to New York, where a banquet would be held in his honor, where he would receive a Tiffany silver tray suitably inscribed. To make this all happen, the journal provided lodging for scores of distinguished guests in the nearby Hilton and secured the banquet hall at the Metropolitan Club.

I've not done Daniel Scot justice, but you can get a good picture of the man on some YouTube videos. In one, he gives credit to his parents for tutoring him in the Scriptures in his childhood. But he couldn't share the gospel with his fellow Pakistanis, for Islamic nations criminalize such behavior, since it appalls and, arguably, terrifies them. Many Christians have been beaten, imprisoned, and martyred. Scot even had a classmate try to kill him in the twelfth grade when he spoke with him about salvation, and Blasphemy Law 295.c carries with it a death sentence—death by hanging.[26]

In another video, "Sharia Down Under," he speaks of the way Muslims use secular humanists to suppress the Christian witness and employ strategic lying to advance their cause. He observes, quoting chapter and verse in the Koran, that sharia law is quite inhumane, including the abuse of women and the duty to kill family members who convert to Christianity. He declares that, when cultures institute or accommodate sharia, "we're taking society back to seventh century Arabia." He observed that Christianity and a fair assessment of Islam are suppressed by violence in Muslim countries and by speech

codes in the West. He adds, "Appeasement is like feeding the croco-
dile, hoping they will be the last one's he will eat."[27]

We used the event to focus on the threat of Islam and the folly of
labeling it a "religion of peace," and a day of workshops preceded
the banquet. Bolstered by the perceptive work of Peter Riddell, then
of the London School of Theology, and Mark Durie, an Australian
vicar/scholar, we prepared a booklet called *Resurgent Islam and
the Challenge to the Church* (the content now available online to
registered users of *kairosjournal.org*.) (Durie, as a member of the
Australian Academy of the Humanities, had published academic
papers on the Achenese people of Sumatra and a popular book on
dhimmitude, the Muslim practice of oppressing non-Muslims in
Muslim-majority lands.) In the booklet, we surveyed the landscape
of persecution around the world, unpacked the notions of *jihad*
and *taqiyyah* (strategic lying), and pushed for "reciprocity," whereby
Christians in Muslim nations might be given the same freedoms
enjoyed by Muslims in Christian lands.

Islam in Northern Nigeria

I got a course in the subject in the months leading up to the event by
virtue of a video assignment. Archbishop Peter Akinola of Nigeria had
supplied us a suitcase full of PAL format video tapes, eighteen hours
chronicling the persecution of Christians in the Muslim-majority
North (Housa territory, Boko Haram's neighborhood, in contrast
with the Christian-majority South, where the Yoruba predominate).
I worked through the footage, selecting about fifteen minutes of
wreckage scenes, a secretly-filmed portion of a fiery imam's sermon, and a survivor testimony. Working with a format-conversion
company in Dallas and the video people at Southern Seminary, and
scripting voiceover, I was able to get those images ready for the
meeting.

The video featured a variety of damaged church buildings—Assembly
of God, Baptist, and a range of non-denominational congregations,

with such names as Rhema Living Word, Cherubim & Seraphim, and Light of God—some torched, others battered into ruins, with broken glass everywhere. The devastation extended from Jos to Kano to Kaduna to Maiduguri.

On one church wall was scrawled, "The Christian Will See the Death." A church member, standing in the ruins reported, "They had several types of weapons. Swords … spears … daggers." Another added:

> We tried to lock the gate, but they broke through the gate. They entered and torched the place … all the windows. They really wanted to kill the pastor … Yah, that day, I feel so bad … I was trying to like depend on God that I invite … I put my trust in God that day. Because I knew it was not by might, not by power, but it was only by the Spirit of God.

The scene shifts to a makeshift studio setting, where a man in traditional garb says,

> All the ways for us to be known are blocked. You know, we are not allowed to talk about it in the media, in radio. We are not allowed to print whatever in the newspapers. We are not allowed to appear on the TV. So, these are the ways people will know there are Christians. But if somebody will go and see the number of Christians, the number of churches, one cannot believe it.

After a shot of Catholics turning over sheet metal, exposing the burned body of a priest, we move to a woman recounting the events of May 11, 2004, in Kano: "There is rioting … he never reached his destination … was almost near the house when the rioters met him running about two hundred-plus, they refused him coming out of the car. They burnt him alive inside the car."

Another woman picks up the narrative: "They started beating us and including my husband and also me. They even stabbed me in the leg. We were pleading, begging that they should leave us alone ... They said they could not leave us unless we turn to Muslim."

And a student leader tells of a different murder.

> He was taken away at 12:30 a.m. The reason for his being abducted is that he is the president of the fellowship of students that had interaction with Muslim students on October 9 in the same school ... And on his head were the signs of hard hitting which showed that he was brutally beaten and then his neck was maybe finally broken ... Well, to be honest, my personal feelings are ... sometimes I feel very bitter about it ... and ... I would want to have some physical form of revenge for myself. But, I'm thankful because I have known Christ a long time before now, and he has been able to comfort me ... I wish for them that what we have as Christians, what we have that is Jesus Christ, would be made known to them and they would be able to appreciate, even if they are not going to repent ... that this Jesus, is indeed, a unique personality. My prayer for them is ... they repent and they also enjoy salvation as we have it today ...

> Many people interpret it as ... maybe misunderstanding between just individuals that resulted to that. But putting together what has been happening in this country for the past twenty, twenty-five, thirty years, there has been a pattern which I believe ... has been planned, is an orchestra, because the sequence of events happened one at a time, at a time, at a time in different locations with similarities ... Well, for as Christians ... one of the things I

would like to say is that we should break our worlds of divide and agree unanimously on the issue of Islam and how it is wrecking us, because a few years, when democracy started in this country, there was sharia law, and the Christians wouldn't stand up unanimously to say they wouldn't agree to sharia law ... Some people were shouting and saying, "No, it's not going to work out for our good," but they were consoled and told, "No, it was only going to affect the Muslims." Because there was no unanimous voice by the Christians, sharia has affected even those who are ... not Christians.

Now, that is one. We must be able to be united as one. Two, is that we should be careful with our dealings with the Muslim individuals. What agreements we come into with them, what pacts, what we share, as on social levels, because they use them as devices against us. Well, inasmuch as we will not send them away, but we should be able to make them know that, even though we are not aggressive, we are also wise.

Next, we hear from a Muslim cleric, speaking in a mosque.

If there are terrorists in this country, they are Christian. They are the terrorists. Now they've started what they call democracy. And they even brought soldiers to come and protect it. They will join the army with everything and remove all the Muslims. And they say, "We are protecting the democracy." No, we are telling you, remove all the Christians for the unity of Nigeria.

By way of contrast, the video featured food distribution to the persecuted by the Christian Association of Nigeria, Kano State Branch.

And a Catholic cardinal, with small shepherd's crook in hand, addressed a large crowd of refugees: "There are some of us here who are not Christians and are taking refuge here. God will protect both Christians and Muslims in Jesus' name."

Baroness Cox, Patrick Sookhdeo, and Michael Nazir-Ali

In preparation for the award banquet, I traveled to London to tape a message from Baroness Cox, who'd experienced first-hand, as a nurse, the trouble that Lasker Jihad had visited upon Indonesia. On that same trip, Peter Riddell and I joined in a meeting on England's Muslim challenge, the gathering taking place in a center devoted to promoting Christians missions and revival in a particularly oppressive Muslim nation.

On other occasions, Brits came to our Kairos meetings in New York, briefing us on the incursions of sharia banking, the emergence of no-go zones in such places as Bradford, England, and the *banlieues* of Paris. Our teachers included Patrick Sookhdeo of the Barnabas Fund (who'd lectured NATO personnel on radical Islam) and Bishop Michael Nazir-Ali of Rochester. (One Brit told us the mayor of Nottingham was a Muslim, and a benighted little Anglican church had come under fire. Its parishioners endured both a rock thrown through the window during the Sunday morning service and thuggery intended to chase off potential buyers for their building, leaving Muslims the only ones in the market.)

And so it was that we marched toward the Vienna meeting.

CHAPTER 17

"I've Got a Couple of Guys You Might Want to Meet."
(From Tokyo to BibleMesh)

In 1970, the Hudson Institute's Herman Kahn had published *The Emerging Japanese Superstate: Challenge and Response*. Decades later, an updated version, revisiting the earlier analysis, was published, and Herb London sent Japanese Prime Minister Junichiro Koizumi a copy. Koizumi invited him to visit, and one of Herb's friends suggested he take him a gift, a bucolic, Japanese-style painting, commissioned by economist and Nobel Laureate Milton Friedman. Embedded in the image were lines symbolizing the highs and lows of both the money supply and inflation from 1970 to 2000.

When they met, the prime minister was somewhat indifferent to the painting and Herb's explanation. He was far more interested in reciting his troubles, and that was essentially the substance of the meeting. Then, as Herb was leaving, he turned and said Koizumi could become the "Iron Man" of Japan (adapting the expression applied to Margaret Thatcher, the "Iron Lady" of the UK). The prime minister said immediately, "Stay here!"

He proceeded to call in the Japanese press corps and told them that the American had called him the "Iron Man of Japan." It got great coverage, his ratings went up 8 percent, he was reelected, and, among other things, he effected the privatization of the nation's postal system. And, gratefully, he invited Herb back.

While in Japan, Herb was pointed toward a couple of young men involved in a startup company called Cerego, whose specialty was instructional applications for smart phones, perfect for study on commuter trains. They'd developed courses in English, the flags and capitals of the nations, artistic masterpieces and master artists throughout history, etc. And their offerings had a twist, a sophisticated set of algorithms that enhanced learning by tracking progress and recycling questions according to a rich mix of encouragement, enlightenment, and reinforcement.

In subsequent years, the system has proven useful to a range of groups, from the U.S. Army to Columbia University. The latter adopted it for preparing their dental students for licensure exams, and all those who took the training passed (a record not equaled by those who didn't choose this option).

Much impressed, London joined the board and then brought the company ("two guys you might want to meet") to the attention of Mano, who wanted to hear more. He invited them to his home in New York, and, having read recently in *Time* that biblical literacy was at an all-time low, he asked them if it could be used to teach the Bible. (Herb had suggested this very thing when he first mentioned Cerego to Mano.) They assured him it could, so Mr. K said, "If you can give me exclusive rights to that, I'll invest." They could, and he did. And thus, the way opened for *BibleMesh*.

BibleMesh

As we presented *Kairos Journal* to a range of publics, we increasingly noticed a more fundamental problem. Not only was there a deficit of biblically-prophetic engagement with the culture; there was a shortfall in Bible knowledge and a sense of how the whole of Scripture hung together. As we talked this over, Greg Thornbury suggested, "Hey, why don't we write a curriculum?" We undertook the project, producing what we called *BibleMesh*.

The name didn't come to us immediately. An agency working with us suggested a range of options, which we considered in turn. There were some pretty good ones (and a few not-so-good), but we kept brainstorming, looking for something that picked up on the thread—the revelation of Jesus—that ran throughout Scripture. We settled on a slogan: "One God. One Book. One Story," and before long, the word 'mesh' came to mind. Cerego had used it, and it enjoyed currency on the Internet. *BibleMesh* it was. And the agency supplied us the logo, an abstract Spirit dove with a netting texture. (This idea fit nicely with Archbishop Akinola's request that we think about providing biblical/theological education to the developing world, including his homeland, Nigeria.)

What began as a Cerego-driven Biblical Story course has burgeoned into a far-ranging delivery system for theological training, with distinctly *BibleMesh* offerings, a platform for Zondervan Academic courses, and partnerships with a range of institutions. (I should note, while *Kairos Journal* is free to church workers, *BibleMesh* courses come with a fee, but that money is channeled to a charitable trust devoted to ministries like *BibleMesh*.)

Brian Pinney, our "webmaster," has briefed me on the technical aspects of the platform iterations —not unlike trying to teach a cat algebra—so my account of what's gone on is sketchy. It involves exotica like Moodle, Drupal, code gymnastics, custom plugins, embeddings, and apps. The Cerego testing algorithms are still much in play, but they don't deliver content, so we've reached out to others for instructional material. I've sat in on several meetings heavy in IT talk and have been fairly mystified by the discourse, along with the older KJ originals around the table. The younger guys, even the content writers, were raised on computers and they seem to pick up on much of what flies by us Baby Boomers. (Of course, Mr. Kampouris embarrasses us other "seniors" by grasping the totality of the proceedings.)

Along the way, we've been helped mightily by Nick Ellis (who did his undergraduate work at Union University and his doctorate at

Oxford); by a member of our original writing and editorial team, Michael McClenahan, who tracks and supervises this sector with aplomb; and by Anglican priest John Adams, a genius at computer programming who serves both church and *BibleMesh*.

Let me add a word on a surprise I got along the way. Late one afternoon in New York, I found myself on the elevator with two young, yarmulke-wearing, orthodox Jewish computer mavens who'd been presenting some very technical (and baffling to me) matters concerning the construction of the *BibleMesh* website. After hours in the Kampouris's apartment with them, their boss, and *KJ* team members who were up to speed on IT options, I was a thoroughly intimidated admirer. I offered them a word of praise, to which they responded that there was a lot yet to do ... to which I responded, "Well, we'll just have to get 'er done." They jumped at my remark, "Get 'er done!?" So, I had to ask, "Do you know Larry the Cable Guy (the "red neck" comedian who uses that expression repeatedly)? "Know him! We went to his concert the other night." Talk about a melting pot.

Biblical Story

The basic Bible course turned out to be a very big project, taking several years to complete. Much as we tackled *Kairos Journal*, we farmed out to the team a range of articles and dealt with others that had surfaced in the members' study. Brian would send out a batch of them, and we'd take to the phones for edits.

As with *Kairos Journal*, we used a template as we crafted articles for seven eras (Creation; Patriarchs; Moses; Israel; After the Exile; Jesus; The Church), with four article categories in each —Historical Event (The Flood); Character (Paul); Doctrine (Creation Ex Nihilo); Context (Hellenism). Also tracking with *Kairos Journal*, the articles were succinct and, in this case, began with a synopsis and concluded with a "BibleMesh" feature, tying each piece to the whole of Scripture as the revelation of Christ. (And, as with *KJ*, *BibleMesh* material has been translated into other languages.)

There were some sparky exchanges. I'm pretty big on etymology and semantics. Others were keener on grammar. I can't remember the details, but I was smoked over trying to make too much out of the components of *ekklesia* ("out" plus "to call") and its use in classical Greek to denote a town assembly, to which the citizens were "called out." It seemed to me to be a very promising addition to the article on the church. But what did I know? In another instance, I was grateful to J.I. Packer for his remarks on baptism. I was Baptist and he an Anglican, and we were directing the course toward both groups. Artfully, he showed a way for mutual respect.

In the end, we posted scores of articles and scores more of videos, for which we fashioned scripts. Sometimes we read our own. In other instances, we invited guests to do the reading; they often wrote their own. It made for quite an assembly of speakers, including Josh Harris on Adam; Vaughan Roberts on the Mosaic covenant; Paul House on the Ten Commandments; Phil Ryken on the Egyptian captivity; Ligon Duncan on Ancient Near East covenants; Terry Virgo on Mary; Rico Tice on the Nativity; Michael Haykin on First-Century Palestine under Roman rule; Noel Rabinowitz on Galilee; Rob Plummer on the harmony of the Gospels; Mark Dever on the Trinity; Owen Strachan on forgiveness; Liam Goligher on the Last Supper; Ray Van Neste on Pentecost; and yes, a lady, in the person of our Tricia Marnham, who did a number of videos, including one on Paul's missionary journeys.

Tim Keller of Redeemer Presbyterian Church in New York and John Rhys-Davies, who played Gimli in *Lord of the Rings*, anchored the era introductions. (Incidentally, though Gimli was a red-headed, dwarf warrior with an ax in the films, in real life Rhys-Davies is 6'1" and dark-haired, and he doesn't typically carry an ax.)

One work session stands out in my memory: We'd rented a suite in an Upper East Side hotel and hired a video crew for the day, with full kit, including lights, back-drop screen, teleprompter, camera, sound boom, and assistants. Alistair Begg and Ligon Duncan were working through agreed-upon scripts throughout the day, taking their turns before the camera. But then we ran out of material, with an hour of the crew's time remaining and paid for. We scrambled.

Alistair and I retired to the other room and plugged a voice-recognition-software rig into my computer's USB port. (I'd started using it when I broke my wrist in a faculty-student basketball game and had trouble typing for a while.) We'd tossed out a few topics we needed to cover, and Alistair said he'd give John the Baptist a shot. So he'd speak a line, and I would repeat it, watching the lines appear on the screen.

As I remember, he started in a wonderful Scottish accent with something like "Jun thuh Bopstist wuz uh strehnge mon." (Apologies to Alistair and to Scots in general. By the way, my father got his PhD in church history at Edinburgh, so I've not been a stranger to the charms of this nation.) And on he went until we had a two-minute piece, which I read back for him to edit on the fly. The whole thing took about fifteen minutes, and we were able to deliver a thumb drive to the teleprompter for immediate use. He nailed it, and we had another one in the can. Pretty amazing, in my book.

The BibleMesh Institute

We began with the Biblical Story and then moved to languages, featuring original courses in Greek and Hebrew. But we also developed a platform for courses from other sources—a cooperative arrangement—and then grouped those courses into certificate plans for those who might want a program of study. (The institute is led and engineered by *KJ* mainstays Ben Mitchell, Michael McClenahan, Jacob Shatzer, and Brian Pinney, with the addition of Benjamin Quinn of Southeastern Baptist Theological Seminary as academic director.)

It's garnered interest around the world. For instance, in October 2017 we got word from Manila that Joshua Gurango, pastor of Christ's Commission Fellowship, had taken twenty students through the Biblical Theology course track, consisting of three from Porterbrook

(The Bible in Missional Perspective; Church History in Missional Perspective; and Apologetics) and two from Bethlehem College and Seminary (Systematic I and II, both taught by John Piper). One of the students receiving his certificate reported that he, a pastor, and his wife were leading a group of students along the same certificate track.

A turn through the catalogue shows courses in Greek by William Mounce, Mark Dubis, and Nicholas Ellis; in Hebrew by Timothy Edwards of New Saint Andrews College; in Latin by Timothy Griffith, also of New Saint Andrews College, and Ryan Handermann of the Davenant Trust; on God's design for man and woman by Andreas and Margaret Köstenberger; and on Philippians by Barry Cooper of Christianity Explored Ministries. You also find Old Testament Survey by Douglas Stuart, and New Testament Survey by Craig Blomberg, working with Our Daily Bread Ministries; a course in preaching from the Charles Simeon Trust, team-taught by D.A. Carson, William Taylor, Paul Helm, Philip Ryken, and John Woodhouse; instruction in missions and church-planting from both Crosslands and Porterbrook; teaching on the doctrines of faith-alone, the Holy Spirit, and biblical authority, provided respectively for Ligonier by R.C. Sproul, Sinclair Ferguson, and Stephen Nichols; plus studies on a range of topics from the faculty of Western Seminary, including one on the marks of a healthy church board, team-taught by Bert Downs, David Jones, and John Johnson.

Zondervan

On top of this, Zondervan has selected the *BibleMesh* platform for its academic courses, including Introduction to Ethics by Scott Rae; Systematic Theology by Wayne Grudem; Historical Theology by Gregg Allison; Creeds and Councils by Justin Holcomb; Biblical Interpretation by Scott Duvall and Daniel Hays; Genesis by Tremper Longman; New Testament Survey by Robert Gundry; Romans by Douglas Moo; and Biblical Counseling by Heath Lambert. All of the sixty-plus courses feature the "Cerego Adaptive Learning System," which takes us back to the two Cerego guys from Japan Herb London wanted Mano to meet.

CHAPTER 18

"May He Stay with You?"
(The Monastery-Language Connection)

Just three months into their marriage, Mano and Camille got a call from Dr. Basil Rigas, a renowned gastroenterologist in Manhattan at what is now called New York-Presbyterian/Weill Cornell. He is a physician who now serves as chief of the cancer prevention division at Stony Brook University Hospital. (He'd served as Mano's best man at his wedding to Camille.) He asked if they might host the American stay of an ailing Father Spyridon, abbot of a Greek Orthodox monastery in his homeland, who needed an operation.

The Kampourises agreed, though they thought they might have difficulty in connecting with an ecclesiastical eminence. Little did they know they would be engaged in deep theological discussions late into the nights he stayed with them. A friendship developed with a kindred spirit who believed the church's prophetic call was (and still is) to speak into culture. Since then, the Kampourises have regularly visited the monastery on trips to Greece. And two decades after they opened their home to Father Spyridon, they turned to him and his monastery's priests for help with the Greek instruction channels of *BibleMesh*.

Most of us on the *KJ* team had biblical (*koine*) Greek in seminary, and I audited a year of classical Greek at Wheaton. It's been fun to have a native speaker (Mr. Kampouris) in our midst, one with whom we can naturally appreciate the etymology of 'Chrysostom' ("golden mouth") and 'Polycarp' ("many fruit" or "fruitful"), the 'Hippo' ("horse" town) from which Augustine came and the "watchfulness" (*gregorios*) of Gregory of Nyssa. And we've enjoyed repeating lines from one of their (and our) favorite films, *My Big Fat Greek Wedding*, such as the one where the non-Greek suitor, Ian, is discovered to be a vegetarian. Aunt Voula (played by Andrea Martin) asks in astonishment, "What do you mean, he don't eat no meat?" At this point all family conversation stops and there are gasps. Voula then breaks the silence with the cheery declaration, "That's okay, that's okay. I make lamb."

We particularly appreciate the linguistic gymnastics of the family patriarch, Gus:

> *Gus Portokalos*: Give me a word, any word, and I show you that the root of that word is Greek ... Kimono, kimono, kimono. Ha! Of course! Kimono is come from the Greek word *himona*, is mean winter. So, what do you wear in the wintertime to stay warm? A robe. You see: robe, kimono. There you go!

And, again, this time from *My Big Fat Greek Wedding 2* (in which their granddaughter, Elena Kampouris, the daughter of Mano's son Alexander, plays Paris, the college-bound daughter):

> *Gus*: The Greeks invented hockey.
> *Costa*: Yes. Because what do you play hockey on? Ice.
> *Aristotle*: What is the Greek word for ice? Pago.
> *Costa*: Pago, puck. There you go.
> *Aristotle*: There you go.
> *Gus*: There you go.

As enjoyable as etymology may be, we've discovered that, with Mano, pronunciation is no laughing matter. For one thing, he says, "CARE-os *Journal*. I/we are more inclined to say "KEYER-os." We go with the "kuh" ending for 'Thessalonica,' the way we learned in Sunday School, but he ends the word with "kee," in keeping with today's spelling. And speaking of the ee sound, he insists on using it to pronounce, 'oi,' as in *hoi polloi* and *koinonia*, rendering them "ee pollee" and "keenoneea." And after a personal, five-minute lesson from him on how to say *logos*, I'm still not there. Something about a soft 'g' instead of my hard-g "loggos." It comes out something like an only-slightly-heard "h" or "ch" between the "lo" and the "os." Troublesome.

To better understand the gravity of the dispute, I've turned to finger-nails-on-the blackboard variants in English. For instance, I cringe when a "good ole boy" pronounces 'guitar' as "GEEtar" rather than "guhTAR." And we Southerners used to scratch our heads when President Kennedy would speak of "Cubar" and "Africar." Then there was the time I went for days at a summer camp thinking that the guys from Northeast Oklahoma were from some place called "Mimuh," only to discovered they were speaking of Miami. And you can't get "hooked on phonics" and still do justice to 'Worcestershire' (pronounced with three syllables) or 'Edinburgh' (pronounced four syllables). Pronunciation variants (and transgressions) can be right exasperating, and yes, there was a little exasperation in the room.

Then there's the *Kairos Journal* logo, with the "ICXC." It looked sort of like the initials for "Jesus Christ," but what's with the C's instead of S's (sigmas)? We soon learned that those were Cyrillic S's, characteristic of Byzantine Greek. It became clear that we provincials were, in effect, using a croquet mallet to play tennis with our Greek Roger Federer, Emmanuel Kampouris.

From that early connection with Father Spyridon, a new recorded version of the Greek New Testament is forthcoming, ancillary to a fresh, critical edition published by Cambridge University Press and Crossway. The abbot at the monastery in Nafpoktos, Greece, will do the reading, something perfectly in keeping with his community of "high-tech monks."

As for the Greek course on the *BibleMesh* site, Union University's Mark Dubis takes the lead in academic advising. He's an expert on Cerego testing and proctors the exams. The course itself is more inductive than typical seminary instruction. The students start by reading through John 1-3, immersing themselves in the language, much as one would if he or she moved to Greece and picked up the tongue.

CHAPTER 19
Epilogue

Although this book must end, the Kampourises continue to see God's promptings and act accordingly. As I write, they've just completed meetings with Todd Komarnicki, who produced the movie, *Elf* (starring Will Farrell) and wrote the screenplay for *Sully* (starring Tom Hanks). He's going to help with the Bonhoeffer film, mentioned earlier in connection with Eric Metaxas.

Eric's book on the German martyr enjoyed wide circulation, and he was approached by some people interested in turning it into a movie. But after initial and superficial contact, they'd not followed through, so he thought he'd turn to an agent to shop the concept around. At this point, Mano stepped in to warn him that, on this model, he'd lose control of the story. And then he said he and Camille would like to help him in landing a good scriptwriter, whose work they could oversee. Thus, script in hand, he could approach an agent. (Little did they know that the process would take longer—four years and counting—and cost more than they imagined, but they continue to see God's hand in the project.)

It's been a learning process, supported by prayer through its various starts and stops, dead ends and live options. An early script was heavy on the psychological aspects, delving into motives, replete with flashbacks. The second version was more of a standard biopic, with special attention to the Nazification of the German church.

Mark Coppenger

And now a third approach is in the works. Yes, it's been an expensive proposition, but they're convinced it's worth it, for they've maintained creative independence. Without it, the film could lose much of its Christian flavor, the sort of thing that happened to the Jackie Robinson movie, *42*, and the treatment of William Wilberforce's fight against the slave trade, *Amazing Grace*. And they think they've found in Komarnicki just the man to make it happen. (By the way, he was a star athlete at Wheaton College, Billy Graham's alma mater, where I taught in the late 1970s.)

So, though we've celebrated Mano's 80th birthday and Camille is eligible for Social Security herself, they're making a mockery of the term 'retirement.' As the old expression runs, they'll "wear out, not rust out."

Appendices

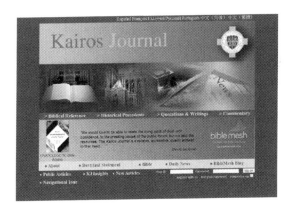

Kairos Journal is centered on approximately 2,400 articles, with thirty-seven topics grouped under eight categories. Each of those thirty-seven topics is treated in four ways—our "quadrant" approach—and each of these ways has its own template. Appendices A-D feature annotated articles, by which we coached new writers.

As the home page indicates, the visitor finds:

- log-in and registration portals

- a five-minute introductory/navigational video, narrated by Ben Mitchell

- a list of foreign languages, through which a generous selection of articles is offered

- the list of quadrants, in all of which the general categories and specific topics are well represented

- a "*KJ* Insights" tab, taking the reader to contributions by a range of guest writers, including Fr. Frank Pavonne of Priests for Life, Templeton Prize recipient Michael Novak, and James Kushiner, editor of *Touchstone* magazine

- a link to the entire text of the Bible, from which readers can access related articles

- a "*BibleMesh* Blog," with pieces by David Roach and others, and a selection of featured *KJ* articles alongside *BibleMesh* updates

- a thumbnail image of the Nelson *Unapologetic Study Bible*, whose commentary is built around more than four hundred of our *KJ* articles

- the *BibleMesh* logo, from which to access that sister site's offerings

- an "About" tab linked to vision and mission statements, bio notes on the editorial board, and endorsements from Christopher Ash, David Dockery, Patrick Henry Reardon, Kent Hughes, etc. (A cycle of these endorsements also appears on the home page.)

- a "Public Articles" option, with several hundred *KJ* articles open to all for a look

- a link to "Daily News"—items on religion and ethics from the press around the world

Once at the site, one click reveals:

- the array of subject categories (Church; Corruption; Economics; Education; Family; Government; Sanctity of Life; Virtue), with drop-downs to the thirty-seven topics (e.g., The Church's Prophetic Voice; Taxation; Parenting; Punishment; Contraception and Fertility; Work Ethic)

- a search feature.

And for those who register:

- access to all the articles, including their foreign-language versions

- a link to print and video resources, including the text of *KJ* booklets on Islam vs. Judeo-Christian civilization (from the Vienna conference) and videos, including those of the Anglican archbishops being honored at the *KJ* Awards dinner, plus another featuring John Piper on the "prosperity gospel" and yet another with Donald Carson speaking on the "Intolerance of the Tolerant."

- the capacity to print and email articles, as well as to save them to a library of personal favorites.

Appendix A: Biblical Quadrant Template
Appendix B: Historical Quadrant Template
Appendix C: Quotations and Writings Template
Appendix D: Contemporary Trends (now Commentary) Template

Appendix A

Biblical Quadrant: Idolatry

The template is: LCAC (Lead; Commentary; Application; Call to Action)

Her God or the God?

An arresting or intriguing title serves the reader well as he scans the possibilities. At least, it should fairly represent the content.

25 nor is he served by human hands, as though he needed anything, since he himself gives to all mankind life and breath and everything. 26 And he made from one man every nation of mankind to live on all the face of the earth, having determined allotted periods and the boundaries of their dwelling place ... 29 Being then God's offspring, we ought not to think that the divine being is like gold or silver or stone, an image formed by the art and imagination of man.

Acts 17:25-26, 29 (ESV)

Since we try to limit these pieces to one page at 11 pts, be selective in your text. Ellipses are an option. We use either the KJV, the NIV, or the ESV.

The English have long despaired of explaining the rules of cricket to Americans, and Americans of explaining baseball to Englishmen. The rules may be stated, but without a clear understanding of the meaning of the terms, the explanation falters. So it is in evangelism; a simple "Jesus died for your sins" may fail to communicate the truth of God to a non-Christian in the twenty-first century. In a world of many "gods," how can the true God be clearly proclaimed?

Paul faced this problem when he spoke to a group of pagan philosophers in Athens. The word 'God' had many

> The **LEAD** should arrest attention and point to what will follow.

idolatrous meanings to the thinkers Paul confronted, for they had manufactured their own gods to meet their every need. Paul countered with an explanation of the True God, He who gave men "everything" (v. 25)—their lives, their continued existence, their social situation. Men cannot make "gods." Just the reverse is true; God makes men (v. 26). The Greeks may have believed they were in control. After all, they could move their statues and idols around the city, but they could not move God. He is the Prime Mover, the one who determines the times and location of every single human person (v. 26).

Contemporary Western man is not much given to carving and casting idols, such as the ones Paul found along the streets of Athens. However, his imagination (v. 29) is hard at work making little gods of the mind. A church member hears a pro-life sermon from <u>Psalm 139</u> and objects, "*My* god wouldn't ask a woman to carry an unwanted child to term." It is, indeed, *her* god and not *the* Living God. A "progressive"

> Since we strive for one-page length, we cannot offer an extensive exegesis or biblical background study. Still, our **COMMENTARY** must be sufficiently careful, instructive, and pointed to advance and sustain the case we're making.

parishioner defends his <u>cohabitation</u> before marriage with, "It's a new day." It may be a new day, but there is no new Ancient of Days. Our "liberated" man may whittle away on his god, adapting him to his emerging interests, but God Himself will not be whittled.

> The **APPLICATION** brings the reader from Bible times to the present. It sets the matter within the contemporary Church or culture.

Desperate is the pastor who must constantly reconfigure his god to the whims, prejudices, and anxieties of the culture. Joyful is the pastor who can, with Paul, proclaim the whole counsel of the Unchanging Creator God, week after week, year after year, throughout his ministry.

NOTE: The black and white version you see here in the Appendix doesn't reveal the blue hyperlinks

> The **CALL TO ACTION** is a word specifically for the pastor. Sometimes we suggest a duty, other times we offer a convicting or encouraging observation. *Kairos Journal* is for the pastors, and here is one place it clearly shows.

that appear on line. For example, in the last paragraph, both 'Psalm 139' and 'cohabitation' appear in blue. Click on the first, and you're taken to both to the text of that particular Psalm and a listing of articles that cite or reference it, e.g., "Embryonic Stem Cells: Fearfully and Wonderfully Made" (Psalm 139:13-16). Click on the latter, and you find links to eight articles, including a Current Trends/Repentance piece called "A Spectacular Fall to Grace."

Appendix B

Historical Quadrant: Pastor, Culture, and Public Duty

The template is EPNL: (Event; Periodization; Narrative; Lesson). By "historical," we mean "more than 10 years ago."

Latinisms and similar marks of erudition can be acceptable, so long as their meaning is clear and they're not overdone. The Journal prizes accessibility, not obscurity.

Simeon *Contra Mundum*

In November 1782, <u>Charles Simeon</u>, the new pastor of Holy Trinity Church, Cambridge, England, arrived eager to begin his ministry. Yet to his horror, he faced the prospect of preaching to a cold, empty church. The congregation, in protest at his appointment,

Begin with a dramatic **EVENT**, drawing the reader into the story.

decided to stay away from services, locking their pews so that no one else could use the seats. Simeon could either quit his post or have any who came to hear him stand in the aisle.

The Enlightenment and the Industrial Revolution had sapped the Church of England of much of its strength in those days. Not surprisingly, the parishioners of Holy Trinity had little patience for Simeon's enthusiastic evangelicalism …

State the historical/cultural context for this event. **PERIODIZE** it.

... They preferred the assistant curate, Mr. Hammond. When at his own expense, Simeon purchased pews for the aisles, the churchwardens threw them out into the churchyard. And when Simeon held a third service in the evening for the poor who couldn't get out in the day, the churchwardens went one step further and locked the doors![1]

> Develop the **NARRATIVE**; tell the story.

The hostility was not only from the congregation. Although a fellow at King's College, Simeon was derided by the university; he was attacked by students and held in contempt by his peers. Students who did go were mocked as "Sims" and, as a result, went circuitous routes to avoid being noticed. For years, the streets leading to the church were the "scenes of the most disgraceful tumults" as those attending church were insulted or assaulted.[2] Students were warned not to attend Holy Trinity, and, when that failed, Greek classes were arranged in one college for Sunday evenings to prevent students from hearing Simeon.[3]

Yet despite these trials and recurring bouts of ill-health, Simeon persevered, staying at Holy Trinity for fifty-four years until his death in November 1836. He did so by recognizing criticism and opposition as the inevitable result of being a minister of Christ. When, in the early days, he was essentially locked out of his church and out of people's homes, he saw "no remedy but faith and patience." Despite great provocation, he was constrained by recalling that a "servant of the Lord must not quarrel" (2 Tim. 2:24).[4] When buffeted by university derision, he reflected on Simon of Cyrene who bore the cross of Christ (Mark 15:21):

> What a word of instruction was here—what a blessed hint for my encouragement! To have the Cross laid upon me, that I might bear it after Jesus—what a privilege! It was enough. Now I could leap and sing for joy as one whom Jesus was honoring with a participation of his suffering ... I henceforth bound persecution as a wreath of glory round my brow![5]

The vicar of Holy Trinity knew where to turn when in trouble—the comfort of God's Word. He would often devote the first four hours of the day to private prayer and the devotional study of the Scriptures.

In 1831, Simeon's friend, Joseph Gurney, asked him about suffering for Christ's sake. How had Simeon overcome persecution and prejudice over the last forty-nine years in Cambridge, to the extent that he now enjoyed such popularity? The wise seventy-one year old commented:

> My dear brother, we must not mind a little suffering. When I am getting through a hedge, if my head and shoulders are safely through, I can bear the pricking of my legs. Let us rejoice in the remembrance that our holy Head has surmounted all His suffering and triumphed over death. Let us follow Him patiently; we shall soon be partakers of His victory.[6]

This piece was done by one of our British writers. In the original paragraph beginning with "Yet, despite," the word 'recognizing' was spelled 'recognising.' Though both spellings are equally valid, we go with the American. Still, we are happy to employ expressions that are more typically British, such as 'whilst.'

Our standard is the *Chicago Manual of Style*, which includes the Bible book abbreviations you see here.

Many pastors today will be suffering for the sake of Christ. They can be encouraged by Simeon's model of endurance, as they fix their eyes on one of those who "through faith and patience inherit the promises" (<u>Heb. 6:12</u>). Rather than seeing opposition and derision as part and parcel of faithful gospel ministry, pastors often feel that they have no alternative but to move on. Simeon's example urges them not

The closing paragraph draws the LESSON for the pastor.

to flee their flock in the face of criticism, but to fix their focus on Christ. Most of all, Simeon's life urges pastors today to "share in suffering for the gospel by the power of God" (2 Tim. 1:8).

Footnotes:

[1] Hugh Evans Hopkins, *Charles Simeon of Cambridge* (London: Hodder and Stoughton, 1977), 36-39.

[2] Handley Carr Glyn Moule, *Charles Simeon: Pastor of a Generation* (Christian Focus, 1997), 58.

[3] Simeon urged the students of that college "to attend the class in obedience to the oath they had sworn to the master and as a lesson to themselves in self-denial."
Cf. Arthur Pollard, "The influence and significance of Simeon's work" in *Charles Simeon (1759-1836): Essays Written in Commemoration of His Bi-Centenary,* eds.
Michael Hennell & Arthur Pollard, (London: SPCK, 1959), 161.

[4] Moule, 36.

[5] Hopkins, 81.

[6] Moule, 167.

While trying to keep the basic text to one page, we allow endnotes on a second page. In fact, one way to keep the main piece brief is to shift some information to endnotes.

Appendix C

Quotations & Writings Quadrant: Abortion

The template for the Q&W introduction is DPPP: (Date; Person; Period; Point)

"A Speedier Man-Killing"— Tertullian (c. 150 - c. 229)

Start with a title, followed by the name and life span of the one quoted. Alternatively, the **DATE** is the year the quote appeared, e.g., '1973' for the U.S. Supreme Court's *Roe v. Wade* decision.

As a preacher and theologian, Tertullian taunted the Roman Empire at every turn, defended believers against the persecution of the state, and often reprimanded Christians for compromising their faith. Famous for his faithfulness (an early developer of the doctrine of the "Trinity") and his failures (his joining with the Montanists—a group who believed in extra-biblical revelation), Tertullian would not allow abortion to remain unchallenged by the Church.

Since we often quote the same **PERSONS** a number of times, we don't need to exhaustively identify him or her each time. Neither do we need a detailed description of the **PERIOD**. Just enough to orient the newcomer. A single sentence or independent clause usually suffices to state the **POINT** of the quote which follows. We don't want the reader to have to guess.

In our case, murder being once for all forbidden, we may not destroy even the foetus in the womb, while as yet the human being derives blood from other parts of the body for its sustenance. To hinder a birth is merely a speedier man-killing; nor does it matter whether you take away a life that is born, or destroy one that is coming to the birth. That is a man which is going to be one; you have the fruit already in its seed.[1]

Footnotes:

Keep the selection as pity as possible. In some cases, the eloquence is the thing, even though the speaker is little known. In other cases, the identity of the speaker or the poignancy of the moment is the reason for inclusion. Also, we try to have good representation across the span of history.

[1] Tertullian, *Apology,* in *The Ante-Nicene Fathers,* vol. 3 (Grand Rapids, MI: Wm. B. Eerdmans Publishing Company, 1957), 25. In other translations, see Chapter 9.

Since we double check these quotes, please mail or fax a photocopy of the original.

Appendix D

Current Trends Quadrant: Repentance

There is no set template for Current Trends pieces. They represent the range of styles one finds in guest columns in contemporary periodicals. They should present the case in a factual, logical, and winsome manner.

> Some CT pieces work from an article or book. Others incorporate a selection of materials which show a trend or phenomenon.

Regret without Repentance

A U.K. newspaper, *The Independent*, asked twenty British celebrities to name their biggest mistake in life.[1] Formula 1 driver Stirling Moss rued the day (Easter Monday 1962) he raced at Goodwood; the crash knocked him unconscious for two weeks—and ended his career. Sir Ian McKellen regretted abandoning his native accent for RP ("received pronunciation") when he began acting. Explorer

> Elements characteristic of the other templates appear in CT articles. For instance, here is a **LEAD.**

Sir Ranulph Fiennes wished he had used mobility kites and had drunk more water during his attempt to cross the Antarctic solo. The most poignant word came from Rabbi Lionel Blue:

> It's an odd choice, but it kept coming back to me. I'm
> a gay person, but I think my greatest mistake was not

marrying a girl who loved me. I was beginning to love her but I didn't honestly know what would happen; possibly my sexuality could have changed—though what we knew about sex we could have written on a postage stamp. But you're in love with a person, not a gender. It could have worked out, and I regret that I passed up the opportunity to be with the greatest person I ever knew: she had integrity, honesty and was completely without prejudice. I just didn't know whether I could be faithful in a hetero relationship.

This is a remarkable confession, with several layers of insight. First, Blue acknowledges that "sexual orientation" may be a matter of *choice*. Whatever one's background, one can choose to put oneself in a healthy context and stick with it—or not. Second, he admits that preoccupation with sex can kill one's chance of true love. Third, he admits that it is not so gay to be gay; he looks wistfully at the heterosexual life that might have been.

Blue reminds one of the "rich young ruler" in Matthew 19:16-22. Lionel has it all. He has authored 17 books, with such distinguished publishers as Hodder & Stoughton, Victor Gollancz, St. Martin's, Random House, and Oxford University Press. He has brought a regular "Thought for the Day" on BBC Radio 4. His resume lists a television series (*In Search of Holy England*), a university lectureship (at London's Leo Baeck College), and denominational leadership (as European director of the World Union for Progressive Judaism). His likeness hangs in the National Portrait Gallery. But his spirit cannot rest.

And this paragraph included a description of the **PERSON.**

Like the rich young ruler, Blue once came to Jesus for answers.[2] He found His followers amiable enough. ("Christians seemed to me nicer than their scriptures.") He liked the parables, but found biblical talk of miracles, an exclusive gospel, and the Judgment to be repellant. Ultimately, it concerned Jesus: "I think the greatest divide between Judaism and Christianity is this. For a Christian, Jesus is the unique and only way that God has fully revealed himself. For a Jew this cannot be." And besides, Blue saw no real need for a Savior:

> And this one included a biblical **APPLICATION**.

> I remember a Christian chap who wanted to convert me. He told me what Christianity would give me, and he told me that it would save me from Sin. Well, I do not believe in Sin. Most Jews think in terms of sins: I do this wrong, I do that wrong, I do the other wrong. I will pray a bit, I will go to a therapist, I will work it out somehow. But Sin with a capital 'S', in the sense of living in it, is just not there.[3]

Yes, Lionel Blue has his regrets, but they mean no real change in his life. He continues to practice and defend homosexuality. Today, Moss would drive differently, and Fiennes explore differently—but Blue marches on in his error: regret without repentance. And in his candid moments, this poor, rich young ruler admits to the sadness that haunts him.

> And here was the **POINT** or **LESSON** to the piece.

Footnotes:

[1] Julia Stuart, et al. "I can't believe I did that!" *The Independent,* October 15, 2003: 2-4.

[2] Blue discusses his contacts with and perspectives in Christianity in a BBC interview.
Lionel Blue, "Son of God: Blue on Jesus," (BBCi Website, n.d.)
http://www.bbc.co.uk/religion/programmes/sog/blue1.shtml.

[3] Angela Tilby, "Rabbi Lionel Blue in dialogue with Angela Tilby," (Affirming Catholicism Website, 1995) http://www.affirmingcatholicism.org.uk/Article.asp?UID=51.

> Just as in the historical and Q&W quadrants, we're comfortable with footnotes here.

Endnotes

1   Shawn Tully, "American Standard Prophet of Zero Working Capital," *Fortune* (June 13, 1994).

2   "American Standard Wises Up: Smart manufacturing methods make it a growth machine," *BusinessWeek* (November 18, 1996).

3   Jack Welch with Suzy Welch, *Winning* (New York: HarperCollins, 2005), 185-186.

4   Larry Bossidy and Ram Charan, *Execution: The Discipline of Getting Things Done* (New York: Crown, 2002), 65-66.

5   Claudia H. Deutsch, "A New Kind of Whistle-Blower: Company Refines Principles of Coaching and Teamwork," *New York Times* (May 7, 1999), C1.

6   Gary Wilkerson, with R.S.B. Sawyer, *David Wilkerson: The Cross, the Switchblade, and the Man Who Believed* (Grand Rapids: Zondervan, 2014), 129.

7   "Quotations on Anguish: From the Legends of Yesteryear," *Bravehearted Christian Productions* (braveheratedgospel.com).

8   Wilkerson, 250.

9   Wilkerson, 266.

10 Wilkerson, 266-267.

11 Wilkerson, 267.

12 Bob Phillips, *Covenant: Its Blessings—Its Curses* (Lindale, Texas: World Challenge, 1986), 24.

13 Wilkerson, 274-275.

14 John Drake, "Karl Tiedemann: Jerry Made Me Do It," *Tom Soter's Sunday Night Improv* (sundaynightimprov.com).

15 "Classic Sesame Street—Susan Sarandon and Meryl Sheep," *YouTube*.

16 Tom Cunneff, "Never Fluffing Her Lines, *Sesame Street*'s Meryl Sheep Is TV's New Dyed-in-the-Wool Star," *People* (January 25, 1988).

17 "Camille Bonora: Muppets Get a Life," *Today's Christian Woman* (January/February 1991), 30.

18 "Jim Henson Muppet Memorial—One Person," *YouTube*. (Camille is third from the left in the closing song, holding Meryl Sheep).

19 Paul Vitz, *Faith of the Fatherless: The Psychology of Atheism* (Spence: Dallas, 2000).

20 Eric Metaxas, editor, *Socrates in the City: Conversations on "Life, God, and Other Small Topics"* (New York: Dutton, 2011), ix.

21 Metaxas, 80.

22 Metaxas, 89-92.

23 Barbara Defoe Whitehead, "Dan Quayle Was Right," *The Atlantic* (April, 1993).

24 Phil Kuntz, "Fund-Raising Race Is Also Part of the 2000 Election Contest," *Wall Street Journal* (March 11, 1999).

25 Michael Ovey, "The Grace of God OR the World of the West?," *GAFCON* (gafcon.org).

26 "Daniel Scot Intro Interview.mov," *YouTube*.

27 "Sharia Down Under: An Interview with Pastor Daniel Scot," *YouTube*.

Printed in the United States
By Bookmasters